CW01664999

Loving Wisdom from the Universe

Teachings from the world of the Elements

Mereo Books

2nd Floor, 6-8 Dyer Street, Cirencester, Gloucestershire, GL7 2PF
An imprint of Memoirs Books. www.mereobooks.com
and www.memoirsbooks.co.uk

Loving Wisdom from the Universe

ISBN: 978-1-86151-832-3

First published in Great Britain in 2024
by Mereo Books, an imprint of Memoirs Books.

A CIP catalogue record for this book is available from the British Library.

The address for Memoirs Books can be
found at www.mereobooks.com

Mereo Books Ltd. Reg. No. 12157152

Typeset in 12/18pt Sabon
by Wiltshire Associates.
Printed and bound in Great Britain

LOVING WISDOM from the UNIVERSE

Teachings from the world of the Elements

The Isbourne

FOREWORD

The Isbourne Foundation, an English charity, was created on 21 December 1995, the shortest, or shall we say the darkest, day, so that only 'Light' would come forward and hopefully in time, other 'Centres of Light' will be created.

There are already many souls who have the gift of 'unseen guidance', and as time goes by and consciousness increases, more will come into the fold. A celebration indeed.

The information contained in this book came into the hands of the Isbourne Centre some 15 or more years ago and brings forward further knowledge from the Elemental Energies who assist our planet and humanity in the great adventure of time-space reality.

The Isbourne Foundation lays no claim to the contents other than the desire to promote the knowledge given through its publishing house, Isbourne Publications (www.isbourne.org).

AUTHOR'S FOOTNOTE

By coming together with a desire to promote "loving goodwill" you may like to assist in creating further 'Centres of Light' around the world, whilst acknowledging those already in existence, beacons radiating light and love through our consciousness to both humanity and the universe. What a joyful expression indeed.

For those readers who feel an affinity with the written word and wish to connect with the Isbourne Centre, please use the QR code below.

CONTENTS

Introduction

Chapter

1. The Outer Atmosphere 1
2. The Earth Energy 3
3. The Life Force of the Earth 6
4. The Inner Earth I 7
5. The Core of the Earth 9
6. The Element of Time 11
7. The Ocean Depths 14
8. The Bedrock Energy 16
9. The Magma Energy 18
10. The Source of Light and Love 20
11. The Mountain Deva 22
12. The Polar Regions 24
13. The Crystal Deva 26
14. The Inner Earth II 28
15. The Mineral Kingdom I 30
16. The Mineral Kingdom II 32
17. The Earth – Connecting Energy 34
18. The Inca Being 35
19. The Andean Being 37
20. The Andean Being - Energy for Healing 41
21. The Water Deva 43
22. The Subtle Water Energy 45
23. The Halo of the Earth 46
24. The Air Energy 47
25. The Winds of Change 49
26. Space 51
27. The Deva of the Heavens 53
28. The Deva of the Planets 54
29. The Lunar Energy 56
30. Beings from Beyond the Sun 58
31. The Solar System 60
32. The Interstellar Essence 62
33. The Pattern of Matter 64
34. New Age Energy 66

35. Communion with the Elemental Kingdoms............68
36. The Essential Being............71
37. The Deva of Ideas............73
38. The Life Force............75
39. The Light............76
40. The Universal Essence............79
41. The Education Energy............81
42. The Outer Reaches............83
43. New Electricity............85
44. New Power............87
45. New Thought Energy............88
46. Harmony............90
47. Cosmic Energy............92
48. The World Energy Force............95
49. The Spirit of the New Age............97
50. The Transforming Light............99
51. The Spirit of the Environment............100
52. The Spirit of Change............102
53. Energy of the New Age............104
54. Energy of the Piscean Age............105
55. Energy Coordinating the Kingdoms............107
56. The Angelic Control............109
57. Energy of the Changes............111
58. The Spirit of the Future............112
59. Prana............113
60. Prana Control............115
61. The Life Force of Mankind............117
62. The Evolution of Mankind............119
63. The Guiding Light of Mankind............121
64. The Spirit of Mankind I............123
65. The Spirit of Mankind II............126
66. The Energy of Mankind............129
67. Mankind's Essential Spirit............130
68. The Spirit of Enterprise............132
69. The Spirit of Mankind III............133
70. Mankind's Purpose............135
71. The Animal Deva............137
72. The Deva of the Honey-Bee............139

IF YOU WOULD UNLOCK
WHO YOU ARE

YOU WOULD SEE
A GLORIOUS BEING OF LIGHT

THIS IS YOUR SOUL
THIS IS YOU

Source

INTRODUCTION

For about ten years a small group in Suffolk, England, has been receiving channelled teachings from a spirit guide who uses the name "Hasim". Interspersed among these teachings has emerged an unusual series of co-operative communications given by the controlling intelligences from the world of the Elements. Hasim himself acts as the channel for these Elemental energies.

It is apparent that these energies are working closely together during the evolution of the present changes, which they expect to affect us all, and that there is an urgent need to develop a closer working relationship with mankind. Indeed, as time went by, the group also began to communicate with the intelligences who regulate and control the evolution of mankind himself.

This is a collection of these communications. The original form has been maintained in order to give a feeling of the power that was experienced, even though this is probably more appropriate for the spoken word.

In the years to follow it will become increasingly important to develop our awareness of, and interaction with, the world in which we live. We hope that these communications will help our understanding of the subtle harmony of these world energies.

1

THE OUTER ATMOSPHERE

We come from the furthest limits of Earth, from the outer edges of the atmosphere. We form the rarest part of the air element at its highest level.

We come to illustrate the conditions at the Earth's furthest point of influence. At that distance the Earth's power is quite weak, and it is only by using the accumulated layers beneath us that we can maintain any grounding or contact with thc Earth at all. Our main influence, therefore, is with the planets, and especially with the moon. We are powerfully influenced by the moon, to a lesser extent by the planets, and more weakly still by the other stars. The sun on the other hand, although very powerful, passes through us without impinging on us.

We are, therefore, lunar and planetary energies rather than solar and it is from these areas that we derive our cosmic influence. We are able to transmute the vibrations from these areas into more earthly frequencies that can then be filtered down through the lower levels of the atmosphere. In this way, the influence of the moon and the planet can reach you indirectly through us. We are like an aerial protruding into the cosmos which is able to tune into these influences and conduct them down through the denser layers of atmosphere to the Earth itself.

However, our role is to act both as a receiver and as a transmitter. We also broadcast the thoughts generated by mankind and the other elementals on Earth. So our role is that of the communicator.

Moonlight is completely different in character from sunlight. The sun provides the life force, but the moon affects us deeply in a different way. It vibrates strongly with the thinner layers of the atmosphere and forms a blanket of vibrations around the Earth to protect and control it. Like silver lining on a globe, it helps to keep harmony within the sphere and prevents energies escaping from it. It transmutes the incoming energies to a level that can be comfortably perceived by man and the other kingdoms. Man would not be able to respond to the direct psychic power from the moon and the planets, Radio transmissions cannot be heard until converted to audible sound by a radio receiver. We act like a radio to convert transmissions into vibrations that man can receive.

The significance of the lunar transmissions is that they influence man's soul. They are soul influences rather than solar influences, Solar energies are direct and man responds directly to them for energy and growth. However, continuous exposure to this energy can be too intense and would stunt growth rather than promote it. Continuous exposure to lunar energy, on the other hand, causes no problem because it is filtered by us and transmuted to a type of power that man can sustain.

At the time of the full moon the sun and moon align to produce the greatest effect. At this time we complement the sun's influence and the negative exactly balances the positive. Man is then able to receive it most powerfully. At other times the influence may be equally strong, but the Imbalance causes you to be unevenly influenced.

We are lunar beings and should respond to the lunar cycle, but because man has become far removed from his elemental roots he does not recognise his 'lunacy'. The elementals, however, react directly, so that animals, plants, crystals and rocks all respond to the lunar cycle. They respond to the harmony that we transmit when the moon's and sun's influence are in the balance at the full moon. Lunacy is the natural order.

We can control the cycles of the Earth indirectly as well as directly. The tidal influence that surges through the Earth affects both the normal tides of the oceans and also a lesser known underground magmic current. In the very core of the Earth there is a flow of magma which is intimately affected by the lunar cycle which is, as yet, undiscovered. Perhaps within the next 10-15 years probes deep underground will discover this and then be able to measure this magnetic ebb and flow. This subterranean tide pulses through the Earth like a heartbeat to such an extent that man is intimately affected by it.

2

THE EARTH ENERGY

We are the Earth Energy. You have met us before, but only indirectly; we came before to illustrate the penetration of the Earth by the energies from above. However, the Earth also has its own internal energies, so we do not simply act as a vehicle for outside sources.

We can give you a feeling of reaction or stimulation from the radiations given off by the Earth itself. You are like a finely tuned aerial – you can receive a broadcast and then transmit that programme down into the physical body, which in turn generates a physical reaction. That is the direct result of the outside stimuli that come from us.

You may believe that you react entirely independently and decide your own activities, but physical energy is not derived solely from within – it is also supplied from outside. This will appear to be heresy, because people believe that the food you eat supplies all your energy, but the human body without the Earth energy would react rather like a jellyfish, wafted this way and that by the passing currents. The energy provided by the Earth is the directional energy. You can tap into this source to achieve your physical and mental objectives.

Activity without direction is wasted and useless. By using your subconscious you can get to know your own individual blueprint, and thus realise your own long-term goals. You are also fed raw physical energy from the food you eat. You then need a bridge between the raw energy and these long-term goals. This reconciliation follows directly as a result of your interaction with the Earth energy.

You have been told how human energy radiates downwards from your feet into the ground and how that energy is subtly transmuted. You create a continuous two-way exchange of energy down through your feet into the Earth. The energy is directly transmuted by our Earth energy and returned upwards around the outside of the human aura, re-entering via the crown chakra. As you generate different energy patterns, the returning energy will be related to what is given out; certain forms of energy are more responsive to Earth energy than others.

Think of positive and negative, or sympathetic and non-sympathetic energies. The unsympathetic energy will become clogged or blocked when passing through the Earth. Sympathetic energy, on the other hand, will become energised and revitalised. Thus the person who gives out the right energies will receive a tenfold increase of energy in return. When you feel listless or aimless it is not usually as a direct result of your diet; it is more likely to be the result of the energy you are transmitting to the earth, which prevents you receiving in return the correct vital energy needed to propel you in the right direction.

This is the nub of the matter. You must address the type of energy you transmit in order to receive revitalised energy in return. For example, anyone can feel depressed or exhausted, but then when offered an exciting opportunity can suddenly tap into a source of limitless energy. Take this example on a long-term view – if you adopt the correct energy radiation you will receive a proportionate energy supply in return.

It is difficult to describe the correct energy output, so you will need to judge it by results. When you feel full of energy, ask yourself what generated that feeling – how did you feel earlier in order to achieve that level of energy? Similarly in reverse, when you feel listless ask yourself what energy you have been giving out.

Each of you can enhance your degree of sympathy with the Earth energy simply by concentrating on it, and your very awareness will make your radiations more sympathetic. For example, when you walk barefooted in the dew your awareness will be heightened. If you are striding down the street preoccupied with worldly worries, it is difficult to become very aware of the Earth energies.

You can also experience our energy by using your hands. Stretch your arms out sideways with palms facing downwards; you should be able to concentrate on the feeling in your palms. You will be placing your hands in the outer edges of your energy aura. If you stand on the ground, in bare feet if you wish, you should be able to sense this subtle energy returning. Your hands are sensitive organs, and as you stand like this you are extending an aerial into the current as it circulates round you and into the eighth chakra above your head. You should feel a small stimulation or tingling. The more you practise this, the more you will sense it.

This exercise is valuable as it reinforces the idea that you are all deeply rooted in the Earth. Your roots extend downwards like the roots of a tree. You are Earth Beings. You belong on the Earth; that is why you are here, Feel your energy extending downwards and along the fissures in the ground; visualise your energy flowing along those lines becoming subtly transmuted and extending outwards, stimulated and revitalised, returning around your energy shell via the crown centre into all your chakras. These in turn respond to provide you with the energy you need.

3

THE LIFE FORCE OF THE EARTH

Deep within the Earth lives the power that provides the energy for life. Unlike the other Earth energies, this power is solely for the benefit of the living world of humans, plants and animals. That is its raison d'être and if they did not exist, the power would disappear.

This energy is like a spring of water that wells up from within the earth and flows outwards into the streams and rivers to nourish the land around. Similarly the inner life force flows outwards, giving out energy, but not forming a two-way interaction. Life can exist at a simple level when removed from this planet, as for example in a space vehicle, but not to the same extent as when in contact with the Earth energy.

This energy provides the continuing Life Force but also the logic or pattern that creates the impetus for evolution. This is more like a generalised form of life energy compared with the individual soul energy activating the body during our incarnation.

On death, animal souls will tend to merge back with the general over soul for that species. Human souls initially remain completely separate but as they progress through many lifetimes they learn to lose that separateness and to become part of the whole. Plants, on the other hand, leave a portion of their spiritual essence in the physical. For this reason when the essential oils are collected from plants it is really the spiritual essence that is being used. This is the reason for the great healing power of these herbal essences.

4

THE INNER EARTH I

Greetings! We come to you from far away. We are not used to this – we will become used to it in a minute. We belong to the Inner Earth; we are not of your kind at all and that is why we are not usually in communication with mankind. However, it is the role of this group to become involved with the mineral kingdom, and as such we come to make your acquaintance. We are not normally inclined or able to do this, but this is a unique situation. Once again you are not fully aware of how unique it is. We hope you will not brush it aside, because it is an invaluable opportunity.

From the very centre of the Earth we come with a power that is not very comfortable for humans. It is a disturbing power, the fundamental Earth's energy. We are the flux; we are the change in the Earth's energy which can respond to the energy from the moon and the sun. It is only by using us as a medium that the Earth can generate these energies.

We are therefore the power-house deep in the earth; we are the very core. Through us the energy can be diffused upwards and outwards, but it only permeates very slowly and the effects will take some time to be felt. The ebb and flow from the moon's energy affects us deeply. We are lunar energies; as such we have a spiritual effect on mankind, because we respond to those spiritual lunar energies, rather than the life-giving energy of the sun.

It is therefore through us that people can come close to the Godhead. We are a source of spiritual energy. People who can respond to us learn to become at one with the Godhead. We represent the spiritual urge in mankind that is our role. We give mankind the subconscious urge to become one with the Creator. This can be achieved because mankind responds to the energy which we radiate from the core of this earth.

Visualise, therefore, the ultimate Source transmitting Light to the moon, which then transmits an energy to which we can respond. Our response in turn creates a different energy, which radiates outwards and can he sensed by mankind, even though he cannot respond directly to the original source.

So we are the vehicle for the spiritual element in man. We are not the same as the rock, or mineral energy as such. We are the core, we are from the ultimate centre of the earth; we are not like the crust, which has a different energy. We use the crust. We radiate our energies out through the crust, but we are not the same.

We are relatively impersonal, and we do not become too involved. Man's thought processes are such that he responds to us, but this is not a two-way response. We are more like a fundamental background radiation, which exists whether mankind chooses to respond to it or not. Even if mankind ceases to exist, we shall still radiate. Mankind's activities really cannot penetrate that deeply, so we are impersonal and unconcerned – not apathetic, but not involved with man's activities out on the perimeter. Nuclear explosions, for example, are contained in the crust and the mineral crust energy is deeply involved, but we are behind the scenes. We are simply a source of radiant energy from within. We are unable to interact with humans in the same way as normal minerals.

On the other hand, we are very involved in the changes to come. The subtle energy from the moon represents the generation of vibrations from the new era, and we respond to that. Therefore the radiation we give out itself has a change of pitch. We can radiate out to mankind a feeling for the spiritual which is subtly different from that which preceded him in previous generations. We can influence him indirectly, impersonally, in a one-way process which can make him sensitive to the new vibrations. To that extent we can be of assistance, provided man can learn to tune to our rather awkward vibrational level.

Mankind has always responded to us, but not necessarily all mankind, He should now begin to respond to this altered frequency. This will not affect all mankind, but the ones who are able to attune to us will influence the others.

My friends, we are delighted to have made this first acquaintance with mankind in this particular cycle. You are almost unique – not quite, but very nearly. We will come again.

5

THE CORE OF THE EARTH

We are capable of being with you even though we are quite unworldly. We belong in the nether regions deep below the earth. We are almost at the core of the Earth. We are the very centre of the world. We come to you with a rather unusual interpretation of the normal vibrational experience. Our interpretation is that of a power-house. We are like a furnace deep in the Earth. Of course, it is physically very hot; however, it is also very hot on a subtle level as well. The heat is a generator, a great storehouse of pent-up energy. The energy exists almost inherently. It is as though it were part of the original condensation of the Earth's energy, focused into a small area at the core. Visualise an intense focus of both physical heat and also subtle energy at the core of the Earth.

The consequence and purpose of this is to radiate outwards. On the physical level the heat from the core radiates outwards to keep the Earth at a relatively stable temperature, i.e. the Earth has a stable temperature regulation like a human body – it will vary only a few degrees up or down, depending on the seasons. The fundamental heat and energy comes from within the Earth and is rather more important than energy received from outside. In just such a way the subtle energies do the same. At the very centre of the world there is an intense focus of subtle energy that beams outwards and upwards filtering through the outer strata to the surface. The interface between the solid and the gaseous is the crust of the Earth, the mantle that you stand on. This is an important point of interaction but the energy comes from within, originally from the core, being transmuted as it passes upwards.

You now see that the energy from the centre is of vital importance to you. You are beings of the Earth. You stand on the Earth and you derive your energy from the Earth. The Earth is crucial to you. As physical beings, you derive physical energy from it but as spiritual beings you derive an immense spiritual energy at the same time. You already know that you transmit your energy down into the Earth and this is reflected back. However, you have not yet realised how your human energy interacts with the Earth energy that we supply. When you transmit energy down into the Earth and it interacts with the Earth energy it becomes supercharged, and transformed into a new, vibrant shimmering haze, rather than a dull slow release. It is for this reason that you can derive such strong energy from the Earth. You do not receive it directly. Your own human energy is transformed by the Earth energy rather than receiving the power directly. Because it is your own, transformed energy, it is harmonious for you and therefore is direct-acting.

The inner Earth energy was a higher level. They brought a different vibrational rhythm. We are not the regulators, but more the fundamental energy itself – our energy is regulated by the pulse of that which surrounds us, thus it is transmitted upwards in a controlled organised manner – but we are the powerhouse. Our energy is controlled by those between us and the surface of the Earth, who can sense and control how much is allowed to be transmitted outwards. The centre generates power regardless.

6

THE ELEMENT OF TIME

We come to you from a great distance. We are from the centre of the Earth, but not from the core. We are from the layer beneath the Earth's crust, the in-between layer. Like the core, we are a permanency and we are less concerned with the affairs of mankind or the nature kingdoms. Our concern is with a much larger timescale. We are concerned with the pendulum swing of time itself. We are like a clock in the earth ticking immensely slowly, that is, in thousands of years. We are therefore the pulse of the Earth progressing through its own evolutionary cycles.

We come to you with the message that you can be a great influence if you can attune to our particular rhythm. We ask you to become aware of the cyclical development of the Earth, although it may be a problem for you to realise the length of the timescale we operate on. We are like an atomic clock on a giant timescale.

You can then become unified with this passage of time. The world of pure spirit, of course, is not aware of time, but the human world is aware of it to the extent that it is trapped by it. We have yet another concept of time; our concept is more like the rhythmic pulsing of the universe and we are tuned to that pulse like an atomic clock. We receive our tuning from the entire universe as we respond to the universal heartbeat. We can transmit that heartbeat into the cyclical manifestation of change. As such we come to you at a very important time, because the clock now stands at ten minutes to midnight. The clock is about to chime and therefore we are preparing ourselves for the next step.

It is not easy for humans to comprehend all this, but you can understand what we are saying and also the reasons for it. For example, you can understand that it is not simply a case of right and wrong – things may change because that is the inevitable nature of the world, but the heart of the universe must keep beating. This is not something that can be arrested – it is inevitable. You understand this and can tell others about it.

So we are the 'middle' kingdom and our element is TIME – the passage and the rhythm of time – both of your time and of our time. Our time is flexible. We do not conform to hours and years, but our time is regular and is in harmony with the rest of the universe. There are many different times, so think more in terms of rhythm. A piece of music will have a rhythm that is fixed, but the music can still be played faster or slower. The tempo may vary but the rhythm is unchanged, so we are the inevitability of the next beat, whether this appears to be fast or slow – we are the underlying rhythm.

You are now experiencing another dimension. Up to now you have been involved with things that were on a comprehensible level. Now you are beginning to communicate with those of us from other dimensions, it is important that you stretch your comprehension in order to understand the significance of what we are saying. We are no longer speaking of purely material things. There are many other dimensions of which we are but one, and you will come to meet them, so it is important to allow your comprehension to be stretched for the next step.

As we said, time is not finite or necessarily measured in hours and minutes, but it is measured by its inevitability and its tempo. We are now at the stage of introducing the next cycle. That cycle is inevitable – it happens to coincide with the passing of a number of years, but that is more a coincidence than anything. It is the inevitability of the cycle that is the important aspect. The nature of the cycle is also important; being cyclical, events will progress inevitably from stage to stage rather than reversing direction completely.

The cycle which is now about to commence will begin slowly. Cycles do not happen in jolts, they begin slowly and accelerate; that is the pattern of a cycle, When the new cycle begins it will not be particularly dramatic. There has been much misunderstanding on this subject. The changes will be step by step; there will be no single point to mark the beginning because cycles do not work like that – they simply go round and round.

You will be able to explain that changes are already happening but they will not necessarily be cataclysmic in the sense that has been expected. Visualise the progressive acceleration as you swing round and turn to face in a new direction. That is what we are – the very tempo of life.

We also have a physical representation which is in the substrata of rock. This is basically the igneous rocks which lie under the recent sedentary layers. It is the rock from the origination of the Earth rather than the molten core or the surface crust. As such we have fissures and openings that allow the magmic energy to flow through us, and although we can respond to this we are not part of it. We can only offer the spiritual influence of the magmic core indirectly because that is not our central role. We normally allow it to flow through us, but we can regulate the rate at which it passes and so control the amount of influence that it brings at any one time.

We naturally work together. All these influences are part of the universal force. Our particular role is to regulate. We are like the balance wheel in a watch, and we control the fundamental pace.

"Perfection" is the inevitability of the rhythm. It beats when it beats. That is perfection because it cannot be improved, because it is inevitable. For material things there is no perfection; certainly there is a conceptual prototype for things like a flower but that prototype itself is only the collective representation of a multitude of flowers of that type ~ the latter produced the former. It cannot be said that one is perfection because the prototype did not pre-exist the reality, Perfection assumes a pre-existence of the ideal. Pre-existence presumes time and we are time.

7

THE OCEAN DEPTHS

We come from the depths of the oceans. We are in the ocean, but also beneath it. We are the very essence of the ocean. The ocean itself is the basic element of water, but we are the underlying element of water. We represent the continuous ebb and flow of energy around the world – it ebbs and flows like the tides. It is also a transmitter of lunar energy because the tides are a physical manifestation of the lunar influence.

It is also a transmitter of lunar energy in a non-physical sense. Lunar energy is an essential component in the power of the ocean. This power is different from the power of water in an inland situation like a pool or waterfall. The power of the ocean has a very serious spiritual content. It is not for nothing that man has sought solitude on and by the sea, People will go to hazardous and uncomfortable lengths to sail the sea – it is not the discomfort that they seek but the power and the oneness, to which they attune quite subconsciously. It is known that people who voyage alone at sea often feel the constant presence of another. The power of the ocean is the communion with the lunar energy.

From the greater depths of the ocean we provide an even more intense power. We provide the power for the continuous creation of matter itself. Thus, on the surface there is the spiritual element of the moon but deeper down, there is a quite separate creativity. It is from the depths of the ocean that the continents are formed. It is from the depths of the ocean that the minerals are formed. It is the continuous up-welling from the depths of the earth that makes the magma flow out into the ocean troughs. Similarly, from the depths of the ocean creative energy is continuously rising. It rises into 'the ocean above and is dissipated by the tides to the different continents. The creative energy of the world comes from the deep. We are that energy. We are the basic form of creation – on this Earth.

We also come to you with a much deeper message, As the oceans are capable of great things, it will be important in the future for mankind to attune to it. It is not an accident that this island is surrounded by sea. You will find that islands will become important places for communion. Like mountains, islands will become centres of spiritual regeneration. Those areas in contact with the ocean will have a special part to play. Mankind will learn to use this and there will be a natural migration towards the coasts.

The oceans also have a role to play because they are able to transmute many of mankind's negative elements. It is not simply physical pollution that is cleansed by the oceans. You should rightly be concerned about pollution of the ocean but it has a power to remove mankind*s negative emotional pollution. The oceans will be absorbers of this etheric pollution) or mental garbage.

The world of the ocean is very complex. We are the undercurrent from the deep.

8

THE BEDROCK ENERGY

Beneath the sea there is another energy which differs from the ocean energy. It is a submarine and subterranean energy which is primarily concerned with the formation of the continents. It is now known that land masses are formed by magma welling up from the core of the Earth into the deep trenches of the ocean. We are the energy that creates continents in the form we choose them to be. In the material world we are the ultimate energy for creation. Our responsibility is primarily the formation of matter, and we are little concerned with the non-physical world. A flow of matter from the core wells upwards and outwards to form the continents. This produces the channel by which matter can be utilised on Earth because the continents are the main habitats for physical life. Certainly there is much life in the ocean but without the land mass there would be no progression or evolution of life.

That is the physical level, but on a less obvious level this energy also supplies permanence. The other energies encountered so far are intermittent or momentary, but we are a more permanent energy. We form a continuous background pulse of energy to generate the creative purpose of the material world. We form the vehicle through which the other energies can express themselves, by creating the physical environment in which they can take place.

The permanence of this energy is important. In the past, when there were serious upheavals, this energy helped to sustain and regenerate life by providing a continuing physical environment. This energy is of particular interest now, because man has already seriously destroyed much of his physical environment and may himself become a victim of the upheavals. This would seriously reduce the amount of life that could be expressed at any one time. It will be through our energy that the material world can continue to exist, and so allow life to continue.

The other Earth energies are less concerned about physical life itself, whereas for us it is central. For example, underground nuclear explosions cause disturbances on a psychic rather than a physical level and so do not affect us directly.

So the prime function of the bedrock energy is to supply permanence, like a flower bed, to allow the seeds of regeneration to continue life on Earth.

9

THE MAGMA ENERGY

We wish you to know that we are probably the deepest level in distance from your own vibration. We come to you from the molten layer within the Earth. You have met the core of the Earth, you have met the lower levels and the upper levels; we are the molten level, we are the magma, the flux, the ebb and the flow. You have heard that we are influenced by the moon; it is true. We are that essence within the Earth which forms the vital link with the spiritual aspect of the moon.

We are a subterranean powerhouse for a very rarefied power. We offer an extremely subtle level of energy. We ebb and we flow with the cycles of the moon – that is our very heartbeat. It is self-evident that our subtle power is similarly in tune with the lunar cycle, but you may perhaps be misled into believing that the energy you feel at certain stages of the lunar cycle comes directly from the moon – mostly it is not so. Mostly the response which the living world has to the moon is from us. We supply that infinitely subtle pulse of the life force.

When we say life-force, we must qualify it because we are not a generator as such; we are a regulator, we are the circadian clock, we are the rhythm, we are the cycle. We are, of course, not the same as the Deva of time, but we provide the heartbeat of the living world. We give the living world its spiritual heartbeat, but this is not on a physical level; it is on the subtle spiritual level that our effect is felt.

The consequences of this can be felt within the mineral kingdom. The mineral kingdom will have cycles of greater sensitivity, of greater activity, of greater power, and these are honed and tuned by our energy. Similarly, the plant kingdom will evolve in cycles controlled by the lunar energy. The sun provides the direct growth force but we, the lunar cycle, control the rate of that development. It is no use having great bursts of development without the spiritual aspect being added in. It is for this reason, of course, that artificially forced vegetables may be physically nutritious but are spiritually empty. Bear that in mind.

On the level of the animal kingdom the response is even more direct. The animals have a very pronounced lunar cycle. Their activity and rest cycles, their growth and consolidation cycles, are all intimately linked with the lunar cycle.

It is for this reason that the magic number thirteen is important. It is our number because it is the number of lunar cycles in a year.

We offer this to you as a very important stage of evolution. You can attune to this power by a conscious level of application. You can feel it but you can also be a channel for it. You can benefit from it yourselves of course, but you can offer it to the rest of mankind; you can offer it to others who are maybe cut off from it. The way to do this is by simply offering yourselves as a channel – the rest will be taken care of. You do not have to be physically or consciously involved; you simply hand over yourselves as a vehicle and the power will flood through you and into the rest of mankind.

It is the spiritual evolution of man which is at stake. Remember that you are going through a cyclical change. Remember also that you, as mankind, have been through these cyclical changes before; you have been through the same stage in the cycle. It is important, therefore, that mankind recognises that this is an opportunity. Being at the same spot as he was before, he has the opportunity either to repeat the same mistakes or to avoid them and progress (and go on to make different mistakes, but that is progress).

So, by becoming aware of the lunar energy which we dissipate upwards and outwards through the Earth, you are offering yourselves as a channel for our energies, Our energies are the ultimate make-or-break. If mankind chooses to become aware of the energies we offer he has the opportunity to progress up one level of the cycle. If he chooses to ignore them he will be held on the same cycle to repeat it again. You, my friends, can be the instrument or the trigger to enable him to step up one level of the spiral.

We thank you. We thank you also for what you will do in the future.

10

THE SOURCE OF LIGHT AND LOVE

As you can hear, we do not have the power that many of our other associates have – we are an extremely gentle force. We come to you with great love. That love is the source of all love. We are the ultimate source of light and love.

You have heard from those who generate the love and the light. They are the building blocks of the light, and the ultimate essence. But we are that love expressed. So they may have been the source, but we are the expression. We are the forms it takes. We form the love and the light; we are the expression of the thoughts of individuals; of groups of people, and of whole species.

We reflect that love and light in a very subtle way because we have a direct link with the Earth energies. Normally you would not expect the Earth energies to be the creators of love, but we are an expression which is reflected through them. So, complicated as it seems, we are a diffused energy which is drawn from the Earth like a nutrient, like moisture drawn up from the soil.

We are able to express that power and that energy through the thoughts and actions of humankind, so the love and the light generated by mankind's thoughts and actions has a very direct and immediate reaction within the Earth. That may not be something you had expected.

So, my friends, you will now realise the importance of the Earth energies with which you are all so intimately connected, and in particular as a group. The significance of your connection with these Earth energies is that they, almost alone, are able to give you that immense source of power and love which all men ultimately use for their life force.

It has an interaction with the earth forces which has not been expected and has not yet been understood or fully utilised. In the past the source of love and the power of love has been used, but on a very narrow wavelength – the human wavelength. We are saying that this love and light is a power with an almost infinite waveband. These can be used in addition to that rather narrow waveband which has mainly been utilised in the past.

You therefore have a unique opportunity to take that power and generate a two-way interaction. You have heard of this before, a two-way interaction with the earth energies and the human energies – the two polar opposites, human and mineral.

Now, by holding that power in mind, by making the mental connection, by issuing love and feeding it into the mineral kingdom, down into the fissures, by sinking and slowly enveloping yourself into the mineral kingdom and drawing down your love with it, you are building a root structure which will spring up elsewhere with renewed vigour and reinforced energy. It is rather like planting a plant. You force your love down into the mineral kingdom but it will then sprout up again all over the place with tremendous vigour and energy and you will be nourished by it.

We already indicated to you that mankind has a connection with the mineral kingdom in his lower chakras, beneath the feet, and they connect above the head in a great egg shape. We are suggesting that the whole love energy operates on a similar but hugely increased scale. That is to say mankind feeds energy into the mineral kingdom, into the Earth, and receives a redoubled energy in return, which is the primary love, and the light source by which you are all directed.

You now have the chance to take that love energy and create a force which is a hundred times greater than that which has been used in the past. We would now like you to try to practise that. We would like you to walk on the Earth, send your love down into the Earth and feel your love being received by the Earth. Draw back that energy with redoubled force and when you have done so, you know that you will then be entitled to utilise that love and Light for greater purposes – the purposes of love of course, those of healing, of service, and of true love.

We would ask you therefore to develop this area. It is not very widely used. It is not very widely understood. It is hard to comprehend. We suggest that you have the power to do so and now also the instruction, the understanding and the methodology to utilise it. We would suggest that you take the chance to do so, as individuals and as a group.

11

THE MOUNTAIN DEVA

We are the Deva from the mountain tops. We are rather special and do not normally live in this part of the world. We are a part of the Earth Deva, an important part because the Mountain Deva is quite different from the normal Earth energies.

It has always been known by mystics throughout the ages that the mountain spirit is of a different vibration from that of the lowland. The reason is that we have a specific function.

Because we protrude above the ordinary Earth level our function is to radiate Earth energies out sideways. Normally Earth energies only radiate vertically upwards, and only affect the local vicinity. The Mountain Deva however has the effect of being a beacon and can radiate power over many hundreds of miles. Therefore we function specifically as a beacon of light. The energy radiated from this mountain beacon is especially for the mystical element in man. It is not surprising that monasteries and mystical centres were frequently built in the mountains.

The mystical element in man is that part of him which is able to tune into his Christ vibration. The Mountain Energy is able to stimulate the response to the Christ energy. You understand that in the coming new age this will be particularly important. Thus we, the Mountain Energy, have a special role to play. We are able to stimulate in man that particular sensitivity to the new age.

In the next few years you will find that man, as he begins to awaken, will feel the need for us and will make treks or pilgrimages to the mountains for this very purpose. It is something which will be felt keenly by those who have started to wake up. We are able to supply the energy they seek. It will be like opening their eyes to become sensitive to the vibration of the new age.

For those who are not particularly awake, this power feels strange and as such it may be felt as a menace. This is because it is so unfamiliar for them. However, those who have started on the path will recognise it in a totally different light. It will seem one thing to some and quite different to others. In the mountains you sometimes feel that, in some way, mankind is an intrusion. In this case it depends on the intention. Those who are beginning to awaken will be there with a commitment. Others without that purpose might be felt as an intrusion. As the years go by more people will become aware and therefore it will become less of an intrusion and so we do not resent their presence.

The desire to be in the mountains will become strong for you all. The energy is specifically for the mystical side to man. In order to tune into this energy you must meditate, because that is the door to that aspect of man. If you meditate in the mountains you will find the results will be quite spectacular. It will be like meditating on a pile of supercharged crystals. Each of you has had at least one life in the mountains and therefore has had experience of this energy but none of you has yet had the awakening combined with that energy. This combination will be much more powerful than ever before.

12

THE POLAR REGIONS

I am one of the Polar regions. We come to you from the North Pole. The North and South Poles are negative and positive expressions of the same energy. We can give you considerable insight into the workings of the polar regions and the effect that they have on the rest of the world.

The polar regions are very special and have a great power which is manifest in the electrical activity seen as the Aurora Borealis. The physical explanation of the manifestation is as an electrical discharge. However, the reason for this discharge is because we sometimes need to give an extra boost to the world. We give this boost on an indirect level because we can provide guidance. We are like the compass of the world. We give the world a direction which is recognizable to the Devic forces and to which they can respond in harmony. They can respond simultaneously to become as 'one' rather than separate individual forces.

Thus the power of the polar regions is that of a communicator and harmonizer for the other Devic forces. You can now see that we are important because the Devic forces become more much more powerful when acting in unison. The power gains strength disproportionately – visualize the effect being the square of the number involved rather than merely the sum total. Imagine the effect of an orchestra at is finishes tuning up and starts to play; the power suddenly becomes immense – independently the instruments make a cacophony.

This we come with a special purpose. Naturally, this is concerned with the changes, but our role is not to precipitate these changes more than the other device forces need to work in harmony to respond to the changes. So, our role is more concerned with their response, rather than precipitating the change itself. Once the change has started it is the response of the Devic forces, acting in unison, that becomes important.

The next stage is the evolution. The Devic forces themselves are powerful forces for evolution because they control the animal, vegetable and mineral kingdoms. Thus, initially the change is not triggered by us, but we then orchestrate the response and develop the evolution from that response. You will find that the polar regions will become highly active after the changes have begun rather than before. The changes have now commenced, but the polar regions have not yet become active. The changes are in the initial stages. They will be orchestrated by us as they get more fully under way. The initial change will produce the cacophony, but once the chaos has wrought sufficient havoc, we will be the harmoniser, to bring about a true evolution on the subtle level. Otherwise the drama would be pointless.

In previous eras the change of the actual polar alignment has been as important as the orchestration. This time this will not be necessary. The polar changes this time will be more a matter of pulsations. The polar magnetism will start to pulsate with increases and reductions in strength. There will be strange local variations of magnetic force developing in specific areas as a result of these pulsations. It is the rhythmic pulsating effect that will precipitate the 'harmonic' changes in other areas.

We are from the Poles. For this reason we come to you on the summer solstice.

13

THE CRYSTAL DEVA

We come with a gift for you – we are the crystal Deva. We come because we are to work with you a lot. We can now begin ~ it is time to start.

Of course we know that you are involved. This is the reason that Hasim has been with you. He is involved because of the work that we have to do together – we will be as one. We have much to achieve and it is important – the planet needs us. We must start this year and then continue without ceasing. This is something that we will do together for the rest of your lives and it is central to your work. It will be the very raison d'être of all your work and healing. Without us you would be like a cork tossed on the waves, but with our help and focus you can achieve miracles. Nothing less will be required. You will know when the time is right.

The first stage is to start to work with us. Learn what you can, become familiar with us, develop what you can, accumulate crystals, start to train both yourselves and the crystals; you will be given all the information you need – you will be able to ask anything you need to know about the use of the crystals.

This is the beginning of great things. We are privileged and honoured to be with you. The reason for the miracles is the very continuation of life on the planet. The next stage will be traumatic, and will affect people deeply. Only with the healing that you can give can the transition be made. Without the healing everything will fall apart into total schism. Only with the amplified healing that you and others can give can the transition be made in harmony, one kingdom with another. Without it there will be chaos.

Milky Quartz is a reflection of the clear. Milky can be made clear and vice versa, therefore you could use two clear crystals and the result would be the same, but the effect on one crystal would be transmitted to that of the milky crystal. There are many types of crystal and all have their specialisation, but most crystals can do the work of the others to some degree, so you do not need to hesitate if you do not have exactly the right types. The most important element is the mental condition that you supply.

The Light from the crystals is immense. Use your own intuition to select the crystal which is correct. Have no regard for the physical dimensions, other than what is pleasing to you. The strength comes from the unity between your mental process and that particular crystal – that combination provides the strength rather than the size or shape.

The success or failure of any human venture depends to a large degree on the positive affirmation that you bring with you. If you approach the issue knowing you are likely to fail, then you will probably do so. The crystal can focus those thoughts and magnify them. Thus you will achieve things easily only if you bring that positive state of mind with you. If you do so, you can achieve ten times the amount with the help of the crystal. The crystal can amplify this state of mind if you are fully aware and tuned into it.

Crystals will need cleaning if you have brought negative emotions along, If you have allowed anger or resentment to dominate your thoughts, then the crystal will absorb those and exaggerate them. So it behoves you to be very aware of the mental state that you supply! Crystals are not things to be allowed to fall into the wrong hands. The potentially negative affects are as strong as the positive. You may well encounter small numbers of people using them for negative purposes. The way to overcome them is by working as a group, and as such, working with a group of crystals, you will be totally invincible. This is something you should eventually be aware of, but do not concern yourselves about at this stage. Do not repeat the mistake that was made last time (in Atlantis).

We will come among you often but we will be with you always. There is a great power and that power is you – use it!

14

THE INNER EARTH II

We are the Earth energy. We have been before in a different guise but we represent the universal Earth energy. We have expressed ourselves in part before, but this manifestation is the total mineral kingdom. We come because the energy involved is working towards a particular evolution which this group can understand. We suggest, therefore, that it is time that this group made a distinct change in its approach to the mineral kingdom.

You know that it is possible to communicate through the use of crystals. You also know that it is possible to create the Light and interpenetrate the surface of the Earth and the mineral kingdom with your own auric field. You do this already at your meetings and in your thoughts. However, as time evolves and changes, there is now a need for a more positive and conspicuous evolution – a more conspicuous communication, and harmonisation between your own bodies and those of the Earth.

We would like to suggest that you form a consciousness with the mineral kingdom which is very deliberate and well thought out. This is not just a random sensation. We would like to suggest that every day in the course of meditation you form a deliberate conscious connection with the mineral kingdom. Allow yourself to leave your own normal physical bodies, allow yourself to slip downwards into the mineral kingdom. As you go down into the mineral kingdom, learn to experience the emotions that we will transmit to you, learn to absorb the emotional and spiritual Earth energies. Interpenetrate the crevices of the mineral kingdom. Draw up the energies that we can give you. But as you return upwards back to your normal waking state in your physical body, you will find yourselves recharged and rekindled with a type of energy that you will not have experienced before.

This will give you an understanding and a harmony with the mineral kingdom which you will be able to transmit to others. This will take place on a subtle level and it will not be necessary to communicate it with us – it is almost incommunicable. You will not be able to describe what you feel easily, but the fact that you have soaked up the energy will allow you to transmit it amongst your fellow men relatively simply.

You will have already made the necessary recipe, as it were, to cook this particular energy to make it palatable and absorbable by your fellows – those with whom you come into contact – and they will then become supercharged and electrified by the Earth energy, which otherwise would have been inaccessible. Like this you will find your own oracle. You can each of you do it. I look forward to working with you, my friends.

15

THE MINERAL KINGDOM I

We are a new energy for you. We have the energy of the American Indians. The Indian people used an energy which was unique to them. They utilised the energy of the Earth Kingdom, but in a very special way. When they related to the Earth, which they called "Mother Earth", they used a very particular method of enhancing the mineral energy.

It is now time for the method of using this energy to be learned by you and the other societies outside that original Indian enclave. You have a great power at your fingertips. It is used by taking the fundamental Earth energy – the universal mineral energy, if you like – and refining it to a level which is much more easily absorbed by mankind. The refining process takes place by the input of human mental energy. So, with rituals and ceremonial functions and by mental attitudes, the Indians were able to transmute the Earth energy to a healing energy for mankind.

You can achieve the same thing, albeit without formalised rituals, by bringing a very deliberate focused mental intention to bear. By drawing up the energy from the mineral kingdom into the atmosphere, as it were, you are able to refine that energy with your own mental processes and to absorb it and to allow others to absorb it. Once you have learned this in your group, you will be able to prime the stage in advance, and then utilise the power as a tremendously powerful healing tool.

Visualise the situation where you will create an energy ring from the mineral kingdom which is transmuted into a new subtle form which humans can then absorb. This will give you a healing ability which has so far been denied to you. You could bring in your patients and allow them to breathe in that powerful healing force. It will allow you to heal dramatically those mental states which might have eluded your rather more conventional approach.

I therefore suggest that, next time you meet, at the beginning of your session, before you start to meditate, you form the intention to draw up the energy, to transmute it and leave it ready to be used – either absently or for anyone in the room who needs healing. Try it the first time and we will come again to follow up any problems which you encounter, or give any further information you need.

16

THE MINERAL KINGDOM II

We are the mineral kingdom. We work together with the Devic kingdom to a great extent. We have been to you before, but in a different guise. This time we come as a complete expression; this time we are the overview; this time we have the totality. We are the mineral kingdom. We are not just an expression of that kingdom, we are the whole kingdom. Within us we include all the aspects; we include the crystal energy, the mineral energy, the centres, the powers and the different frequencies. We include all the expressions of that mineral energy.

We come tonight very specifically because, as a group, you have the opportunity to develop, with us, a very wonderful, unusual and special communion. The communion we wish to seek is a healing operation. At the moment, there is a need for us to work together. We have looked forward to this time for many millennia. The moment has now arrived, and the need coincides with the moment. You know that the crisis facing the world is stark and real. You know that mankind alone is incapable of solving the problems which he himself has generated. You do not need to despair, as mankind is only part of the equation. However, while mankind is isolated from that equation, he is also the problem. If mankind can be combined and unified with the rest of the equation, he becomes part of the solution.

The resolution we seek is a communion of energy. The energy of mankind needs to be in harmony with the energy of the mineral kingdom. When that happens, the other two energies, of the animal and the vegetable kingdoms, sandwiched in between, will also become in harmony. The reason that our friend asked us to create this great well in the centre tonight was to allow that harmony to begin to commune with you. You are now able to let your own energy join with me – I wish you to do this as an exercise.

Allow your mind to sink gently into the centre of the circle, to sink downwards, down into the well, down into the well, come with me into the mineral kingdom. Deep down, there is a source of powerful energy which you can now feel. The energy which you are sensing at the moment is the fountain, the source from which you will draw this transforming, translating energy. Sense the feel of it, remember the feel of it, sense the spell, the power, the vibrating tingle of it, allow it to become part of you; allow yourselves to absorb it, allow yourselves to take it in and as you slowly come back to the surface you are, each of you, irrevocably changed. You have made the connection. You now need to take with you, out into the world, that transformed energy which you now represent. Everyone that you meet will sense the difference.

My friends, you can if you wish carry out this exercise on a semi-regular basis. As you meet, maybe once a month, you will find that each time you do it you will be recharged. Each time you absorb the mineral energy, the mineral energy also responds to you. Each time you are in communion with the mineral energy, your own awareness is heightened. Take out that awareness, and use it.

Make sure, as you return to yourselves, that you are whole, that you are complete, that you are all back.

My friends, thank you for your help. I will take my leave, and bid you good night.

17

THE EARTH – CONNECTING ENERGY

We are the Earth energies again. We wish to re-establish the connection which has been made in the past but which now needs to be reinforced. We are a slightly different expression from those energies which were expressed in the past. We are the Earth energies which suffuse the crust, or surface layer, of the world, but we are not the energies associated with that crust. We are more like an impregnation. We are like the salt of the Earth, the spice; we provide that hidden extra ingredient to the mineral kingdom, and mineral energies, with which you now need to make your connections.

The spice that we represent is the subtle twist; it is the "extra ingredient", shall we say, which is going to enable you to make the transition. We could be said to represent that aspect of the mineral kingdom which is reaching outwards, and sending out the message to form the connectedness. It is as though we are stretching out a hand in welcome. That is not something which the rest of the mineral kingdom does very willingly or easily. We are somehow the messenger. It is through us that we hope the connectedness with humankind can become a reality. We offer you our hand in recognition.

So, just as your friend was describing the need to use the mineral kingdom to align yourselves, so, similarly, we need the connection with the human kingdom to realign ourselves. We depend on you and so, just at the time when you need to form a connection with us, we similarly need the connection with you. I would ask you, therefore, in your meditations and in the ideas which you spread around that you should include us – the messenger, the connecting force.

If you bring to mind an awareness of this connectedness, and the specific role of the connecting energies, you will find it easier than trying to absorb the whole of the mineral kingdom, as it were, undigested. We will be like a doorman for you – we will hold the door open to allow you access.

18

THE INCA BEING

Greetings. This is new for us. My friend indicated that we would like to work with you. We are an alternative view from the same source – the same truths with a different twist. We come from a remote tribe in the Andes. We have a common link with the mountains and the power derived from them. Because our cultural background was such, we have a new perspective which we hope will be useful. We have begun to feed an unusual power to you which you have not fully felt yet, but you have had some sensations from it which are rather powerful. You will need help in recognising and acknowledging this new power. You are ready for it and now wish to develop with it.

Our responsibility is to channel this power through you and thus to develop it. We feel there is a need in the world for this mineral aspect, which has a multitude of expressions involving all the forces in the mineral kingdom and all forces that can interact with the mineral kingdom. Healing, psychometry, telepathy, and work with crystals are all aspects of that same power – the interweaving of the human weft over the mineral warp to form a common cloth. Hopefully we will be able to work with you over the next year or two to develop these aspects, and we will be happy to come amongst you to talk to you and to encourage you to utilise those areas. It is something which the world is ready for and it is also something which you as a group can understand and develop.

We have indicated in the past that there are not many groups which have this particular aptitude and it is important, if you don't mind, to take it reasonably seriously and to be slightly methodical about the development; be a little more rigorous in your exercise and its assessment than perhaps you have sometimes been over the other aspects. If you don't mind, we would like to suggest that you keep specific notes and a log of the area which we wish to develop, so that you can practise it, monitor it, and get continuous feedback of what you are hoping to achieve, and how near you have actually come.

It is something that will develop very naturally, but as you well know it is very easy to receive a great idea, and two months later you have forgotten what the idea was. Because it is unusual, and because there will be no reinforcement of the ideas from outside sources (you will not read about it in any books), it will be very easy to forget about them and then come back and remember what you were supposed to have been doing, so I ask you to be a bit more methodical in your approach than you might normally be.

Now a little of my own background – we indicated that I come from the Andes. We had our own culture based around these mineral stones. We had a very well-developed gem culture. If you do your research you will find that the Inca communities in the Andes had a lot of gems which were used ceremonially. They were worn on important centres of the body, such as the forehead and throat, for very specific reasons. The degree to which they developed was very sophisticated in a narrow area. They were able to develop telepathy by augmenting man's natural telepathic ability with gems. That is a narrow aspect, used for communication. We wish you to take that basic knowledge and skill and amplify its application, to use it, for example, not just to communicate but to broadcast love. You now see the breadth that we are looking to you for. We wish you to develop this aspect on a very broad approach – that it is more what you would expect in the new era we are about to embark upon.

So, my friends, exciting things ahead. We hope you will feel our own enthusiasm for them, and that it feels natural for you and you are not struggling to generate an artificial interest in it.

19

THE ANDEAN BEING

This is nice. I have come back to you for the second time. I am your Andean friend. My experiences, and my ambitions if you like, are something that I would like to share with you.

I indicated to you that our particular experience was with the mineral kingdom, and that is an area we would like to explore with you. You know, of course, that there is great energy stored in the rocks and that by certain techniques it is possible to release that energy. You, as individuals, can turn the tap and allow the energy to flow out. Stored within the Earth there is an immense reservoir of mineral power and we hope that during the next twenty five years this energy will begin to be used. We say "we hope" because of course it presupposes that the energy will be used wisely; it has considerable power and could easily be misused.

So, the knowledge will become available and we hope it will be fed to groups like yours who are obviously responsible and sensible. There is always the possibility, of course, that the thing could be misused, but that is a risk which has to be taken because the time is now ripe for this extra layer of knowledge to be peeled away and exposed to the sunlight. Interesting times ahead.

The basis of the knowledge of course is something which has been there before in certain tribes and in certain cultures, but by its very nature it has been occult, and hidden. This was deliberate, and it is only now with the change in the world environment that the knowledge is ripe for dissemination. Now, as you already know, the great energy within the rocks is a little awkward and difficult, unknown and unfamiliar for mankind. When going deep into underground caves, when sitting on a mountain top or sitting in some remote and desolate corner of the earth, many people have a feeling which is certainly one of awe, but almost of fear as well. That is an indication of the fact that this is a very strange and unknown energy, and explains why the response is one of fear rather than disinterest or even attraction.

So, the fear is the fundamental problem and a problem which needs to be resolved before any true knowledge can be obtained. The way to overcome the fear is probably a practical one. There is no way to overcome it apart from living through it; you cannot tell somebody not to be afraid. But if a person can experience the thing that they fear and realise that it is a phantom, or something which is not worthy of their fear, then of course the fear will evaporate. And so the first stage probably is to gain an experience with the mineral energy.

We would like you to join us now and sink down with us. Come with me and hold my hand while we merge ourselves with the Earth's energy. It is most appropriate that you should be in this hut tonight, because you are closer to that energy source. Draw round with me into a close knit mental circle and visualise in the centre of this circle a funnel going downwards into the core of the earth; you find yourself being drawn slowly down through the hollow of the tunnel. You are going deep into the Earth, down and down, it gets darker and darker and you are now beginning to experience the power, the raw power of the Earth's mineral energy surrounding you. You are penetrated by it and it has a certain chill, a certain dull, dank strength. But that power is one of immense creativity. As it penetrates you, you will find that you have new sources of energy that were totally unknown in your ordinary human state before. You will find that you will start to have a power. You will find that you grow in stature, you become larger than life. You can feel yourself expanding into the surrounding Earth energy. You are growing with it and deriving strength from it. Allow yourself to expand, feel yourself growing stronger and stronger.

You will see that this Earth-mineral energy is not something to be afraid of; it is something to draw strength from and with the strength you derive from it you will feel ten times the person you were when you relied on mere human energies. You will feel redoubled, you will feel as though you have a double skin to give you that power and strength that you lacked before. Feel the energy that it generates; feel the combination of the mineral energy with your human energy – that is the significant factor. It is the combination of the two energies which is drawing the strength for you. It is not one and it is not the other, but it is the interplay of the two working together. Feel the power, feel yourself stronger, feel the resilience that it builds. As you withdraw back up the tunnel, out towards the Light, up to the Earth's surface, you will bring that energy with you, and you will have it within you and it will become part of you. It will be something which never leaves you because you have assimilated it and you have grown with it. It is like absorbing a mineral into your bone structure – it is there locked into you, a part of your heritage.

So, you see my friends, the mineral energy is there to be used and will give you a power which is almost inconceivable. It will give you a strength which you have not known before. You will become superman, literally speaking, because you will have a radiant power, the combination of human energy and mineral energy, which is unique. It behoves you therefore to decide now how you wish to use that power. That is something that I must leave with you.

As to who I am – I am simply the essence, or the spirit, of an individual who lived a very long time ago. We were a powerful tribe in the Andes, probably two thousand years ago. The situation then was that the old mineral energies of the Atlantean era had been dissipated and corrupted. We became the guardians of that knowledge, and we were able to keep the knowledge. We were a group of people who were interested in and able to utilise the power for a number of different purposes, That knowledge still persists now in a few small groups in the high mountains, in Asia, Tibet, and also in Southern America. That knowledge, however, will not be the source of the revival of the mineral energy. The knowledge was like a candle burning, but that candle will not become the new furnace. The new furnace will be lit, driven and powered by the suffusion of the knowledge through groups like your own. That will be much more effective than trying to take the knowledge from a few closed orders (they are not formal religious orders, but closed groups), because they are not in the habit of disseminating the knowledge and therefore it would be very difficult for them. But they have been the custodians of the knowledge through the centuries. Their role was not that of broadcasters; they were archivists. If you like, they were the keepers of the knowledge and we are the publicists, the PR people.

I am a totally human essence, a human being, but one who has In the past been used to absorbing the mineral essence as well. It is as though you have been like a sugar lump dunked in the coffee – you have soaked it up.

We lived before the main Inca civilisation. The Incas are relatively recent, but of course within those groups there were the guardians, the closed groups of people who also guarded the information. Do not necessarily regard the Incas as a particularly evolved era. Certainly some members had a very evolved knowledge, but it was not common parlance; it was not widely utilised, and not necessarily utilised for the beneficial and constructive purposes which we hope you will use it for now. I hope you understand the difference. The difference is not in the knowledge, but in the use to which you put it.

There are many powerful centres in the world; you cannot isolate this energy and say it exists in one place but not another. The significance of these power points is that they are places where the energy is accessible rather than that it exists.

You may feel that it would be more concrete if you were working with somebody in a complete trance with no possibility for him to mingle with the events. I say that what you are doing would not be possible under those circumstances. It is only because we are able to merge or mingle that this communion with the mineral essences is possible. If you were working with a deep-trance channel, this subtle variation of energy would not be possible.

My friends, thank you. We look forward to working in the future, because we have so many ideas to develop and so much to be reactivated. Thank you for your energies.

20

THE ANDEAN BEING – ENERGY FOR HEALING

We are your Andean friend again. We would like to talk to you about a different aspect of the Earth energies.

Last time we introduced you to a generalised Earth energy from which you can draw energy and become supercharged. However, .'there are other energies that are much more specific. By conscious effort, you can attune to certain Earth energy frequencies and draw out a narrow band of "Light", for want of a better word. Imagine yourselves as a prism which can bend and deflect that particular colour of Light in specific directions.

In particular we are talking about the power of healing. When you heal you operate on many levels. In one way you heal by allowing other entities (non-incarnated human souls), who have a particular skill, to use you as an outlet. That is fine, but healing takes place on many levels at the same time. If you are careful and specific with your request, you can allow this special Earth energy to become a healing ray as well. You can re-focus that healing ray through yourself to others, and it is a very powerful source of healing.

You know, of course, that by conscious decision you can draw healing from the Earth for yourselves. It is very powerful and you can feel it when you walk on the ground; you can become conscious of it by opening your mind, body and soul. Now as you draw that energy up, consciously direct it in a way that.it can be useful. In the same way that you offer yourselves as healing channels for human energies, you can also act with the Earth energy, and you will find that it is immensely powerful.

It can be used either for direct or absent healing, but probably most effectively for absent healing. Normal human energy needs to be very finely tuned to be effective when used absently – you need to have a very clear idea in your mind's eye of how you wish it to work; not everybody has that clarity of visualisation and imagination. However, the Earth energy can be directed more easily and is good at going distances – it is not deflected by muddled thinking or lack of clarity.

So, we would suggest that as an exercise you should try lying on the ground and drawing up the Earth energy into your body. Ask the Earth specifically to draw to yourselves the healing energy which can be re-directed; simultaneously visualise those to whom you wish the energy to be directed, and you will find the results quite spectacular. So this is a valuable extra string to your bow – an additional source of healing. You will also find that this source of healing has a rather specific effect, because it can be used for the healing of the mind. The mind is particularly vulnerable at the moment and those who are suffering disquiet and dis-ease will be helped specifically by this remote control Earth energy. So, my friends, try it and see. You will be quite pleasantly surprised.

The other way to make it work, if you really want to appear foolish, is to encourage your patient to join with you and lie on the ground – not always easy to bring about because it is pretty weird, but where it is possible, try it and see. Alternatively stand and ask the individual to concentrate on absorbing the energy and you can be like a conductor directing energy from the Earth up into them. You can visualise it and allow it to happen. That is another way.

So, to summarise, we have a wide spectrum of energies from the Earth. We introduced you to the white Light which covers all the energy rays and colours, but within that white Light there are one or two specific bands of colour, as it were, which can be utilised for special purposes. One of those is healing and the way to achieve beneficial use of it is to concentrate on the healing energy – ask for the healing energy, and it will be supplied for you. You will be tuning to that specific ray because of your request and you therefore become a channel for that particular ray. Try it – you will be delighted.

21

THE WATER DEVA

We are the fountain of life, both the spring and the well-head. We are the source to which everyone must return in order to fill their pitchers to be able to survive. We are the source for man, for nature, for Earth and the Spirit.

The water is the fountain of life. We can supply power only because people need to dip into this spring. By ourselves we have no power and we can only supply energy as man draws from the spring. The chalice contains the water of life. For this reason the chalice is the source of knowledge, because life is knowledge. The stream of knowledge flows from generation to generation. The fountain of knowledge and the fountain of life are one and the same. This is why the well-head is now so precious. It is important that the water is clear and unpolluted, because if people dip into a contaminated well the impure knowledge will be spread far and wide.

So the clarity of the fountain is vitally important. The clarity concerns you now because you have the power to clarify this water. It is as though the stream is clouded and by scattering finings across the water the silt can be settled to the bottom and the clear water drunk.

The finings we refer to are the practical examples that you set to others. By your example of living you are able to clarify the water of life. It is through the ley lines that your practical example can be communicated to others. To be effective the finings have to be scattered widely and evenly. The refinement of individual thought can be connected via the channels of the grid.

So your function as forerunners is to clear the waters to allow deep draughts to be drunk in the future. This is what you are. The age of Aquarius cannot come about until the waters are refined and cleared. The pitcher must be full of clear water before it can be poured.

When the cleared water is drunk, the illumination for the world can be digested and understood. If the water is not clear the result would be

Montezuma's Revenge! Clarity of thought is the essence and this clarity comes from love, the prerequisite. Following love comes non-attachment to possessions or even to people, and secondly comes active service, which forms the physical expression of the refining thought. Love of mankind must inevitably lead to the activity of service.

You are the forerunners and with the refiner's fire you will stimulate change. After the change the water will need to be drunk, but only after it has been cleared. The water is powerful. As you use this power you are not always aware of the results. The power can sometimes be unbalanced. You must therefore be careful and always check what you are attempting to achieve, namely the love and its inevitable consequence of service.

As the changes start you will find it hard to maintain that clarity of vision when all about you are grasping at straws. The way to keep steady is to return to the source. It is easy to see how a clouded thought-form can become spread, and as it becomes fashionable it can generate a power of its own.

Welcome to the Age of Aquarius, of clear pure water, of true knowledge. But the pitcher full of water is useless. It only becomes useful when It is poured and this knowledge given out.

My friends, I wish you Good Luck.

22

THE SUBTLE WATER ENERGY

We represent the element of water in its purest form, its finest distillate, We are the essential ingredient, the elixir, the 'subtle stuff of water, Visualise water both as a liquid and as a vapour – we are like subtle, intangible water vapour.

We come to you because this 'subtle' version of water is an important element for mankind. Physically liquid water is man's source of life: he needs water to drink even more than food. Similarly the subtle element of water is also vital to mankind; it is the essential nourishment for man's soul. Without it he is nothing, he would shrivel and die away, because without his soul man's body would die.

The element of water and mankind are inextricably linked together – they cannot exist without one another. On this subtle level the water needs mankind as much as man needs water, though this does not apply on a physical level. For man, water forms the chalice of life but the chalice amounts to nothing unless it is used. The chalice only becomes clear and valuable when the water flows freely. It only flows when it is drunk, and it can only be drunk by man. Mankind, therefore, is an essential ingredient in the scheme of things and he is vital to the element of water. While living and breathing, he stimulates the subtle water. He is able to do this because his soul is highly complex and operates on many levels. While one part of his soul can respond to the core of the Earth, another responds to the lunar influences, but none of these facets can function without the fundamental interaction with the subtle water energies.

Water energies of course are everywhere, but they are especially concentrated in streams and rivers. For this reason the energy concentrates in underground streams that form the network of natural ley lines. When mankind responds to these underground ley lines he is actually responding to us, on a soul level. The water element and the ley line system all form part of a highly complex pattern.

Drink deeply from our cup of life!

23

THE HALO OF THE EARTH

We are another new energy. We are the next stage in the development of the etheric band around the Earth. You have heard from all the Devic energies within the Earth. We are a band of energy outside the immediate environment of the atmosphere. You can visualise us as a halo around the Earth, a band of energy, thicker and stronger in some places than others, but by and large we are like a shell around the Earth. We are a long way further out than the atmosphere. We almost reach as far as the moon – but not quite. That is the approximate distance that we extend from the Earth.

Like a shell we provide protection. We protect the Earth from the powerful energies from the rest of the Universe. The Universe has very varied patterns of energy and not all of these can be beneficially absorbed and used by the Earth. Thus we are also like a filter that can allow the beneficial energies through and filter out those energies that would be too disturbing or indigestible for the Earth and its inhabitants. That is our prime role,

We have an additional function, which is to create a power. We receive energies from outside, and actually use them to create a power ourselves. We can beam down shafts of energy that we have been able to transmute from outside. That energy is the source of many of the other energies who have been communicating with you. They are able to tap this source from us and utilise it for all their various purposes. They are able to tune into this universal energy to use it on a simple level, to supply the plants etc, and also on a higher level for all the more subtle forces with whom you have spoken.

We are the universal energy source wrapped around the Earth both to protect and to energise it.

24

THE AIR ENERGY

We are the power that comes to you during your Earth existence. When you first incarnate, you breathe in energy. The first breath you take is the most important one. What you do when you take this breath is to draw in the air. We are the expression of that energy. In the past, you made contact with the air element and the Light energy within the air; but we are subtly different.

We are a version of the energy of the air which exists for the purpose of providing energy to the animal kingdom – the animal kingdom can breathe in this aspect of the air energy. Certainly, plants breathe air but they do not utilise this animal energy in the same way. They draw their prime energy from the Earth and the air is secondary. Mankind also draws its primary energy from the air. Were you to be sufficiently attuned, you could derive all the energy needed to live from the air – you would not need to eat or drink.

It was indicated before that when you feel weak or lifeless and you are losing energy, all that is required Is to re-establish contact with the Earth energy. That was on a physical level. Regardless of how good your diet is, unless this contact is made with the Earth, you will feel lifeless and lacking energy. You have to make contact with the Earth energy in order to maintain that basic physical vitality. Certainly you normally require a good diet to operate physically, but unless you make contact with the Earth energy you are nothing – a pale shadow. The Earth energy is the vital mainspring (in cooperation with the physical nutrients) for physical existence. However, we are talking about the mainspring for a more refined level of energy. We provide a subtle energy rather than the physical energy provided by the Earth.

The subtle energy is crucial because without it the physical has no ultimate form. The physical body is the copy of your etheric reality. In the same way your physical energy is a reflection of the true, subtle energy which is drawn from this aspect of the air energy. So, as you draw in air for the first time, you draw that vital essence into the physical body.

During any meditation the most important aspect is breathing. If you breathe correctly you will draw in the subtle energy correctly. You can then utilise it on a subtle level. Your subtle energies are the most important: without them your physical energy is of no value ; it is undirected, unrefined and of no real consequence or purpose. The subtle energy gives direction, shape and purpose.

We are the subtle aspect of air that provides this energy for the animal kingdom. As such we have an important role to play at this stage. As you start to experience the subtle changes taking place in mankind and the world during the next cycle of evolution, the only way to draw strength for this new challenge, and to make the correct adjustment, is by breathing in this aspect of the air energy. Breathing will become a crucial function in the future (ie. breathing the subtle energy, not the physical). It will become as important as eating and drinking is to the physical body.

The way to take full benefit from this energy is to concentrate on it, be aware of it. As you breathe, become aware of the energy you are breathing in. As you wish to meditate, first be aware of the energy that provides the force for the meditation. We suggest that you do not need to bother with ancient systems of breathing that were established thousands of years ago for a different cycle of evolution. They had their value and still have value for those who cannot comprehend anything else. However, the aim is simple – the most important function in breathing is to become aware of the purpose of it. Everything else follows naturally. If you are aware of this purpose, you will also become aware of the result. You will become aware of the cause and then the effect. You will become vitally aware of the subtle energy suffusing your subtle body.

I repeat: as you wish to meditate, first start to breathe correctly, with the mental awareness of the effect of this subtle energy rather than the physical act. It will provide you with the energy level you need to attune to the new energy suffusing the world. That will become almost the only way you can guarantee to become attuned to the new cycle of evolution.

25

THE WINDS OF CHANGE

We are the wind. We can only occasionally be seen by man. We are a particular pattern adopted by the element of air; we only exist when the wind blows, and we form a structure or network .which is certainly visible to some of you. Ask to see, and some of you will learn to see the grain or grid pattern we form. There is a small pattern and also an over-grid.

We construct this grid deliberately because the purpose of the wind is to bring about change. Our effect is to bring about changes in the natural environment and the cycles of nature. On a simple level, we cause the seeds to be scattered, the old and weak to be removed, the rains to come and the sun to return. Without the wind there is no change, no weather would vary and no germination would take place.

On another subtle level, the air is the medium of Light. As such, we are the transmitters of Light to bring about the changes. We are able, therefore, to bring powerful injections of subtle 'Light' into the world at certain times and seasons. On this level, we are the instigators of seasonal change. When plants respond to seasonal change (even where the weather seems unseasonal) it is because they react to the change of frequency that we bring. They respond not only to physical Light but, more particularly, to the subtle 'Light' energy.

Because we are the instigators of seasonal change on a fundamental, evolutionary level, we also instigate change for mankind and the world. We infiltrate new patterns of subtle 'Light' into the world just as we instigate changes in the normal pattern of the seasons. Therefore, it is we who will precipitate the next cycle of evolution – the 'winds of change' .

We can create a wonderfully beneficial effect. In nature we remove the chaff and dead leaves of one generation to bring in the new spring. The winds of change will blow away the dead leaves of the older generation of ideas. We bring the Sunshine and Light of the new era: the new buds will respond and grow in strength and confidence as they feel the warmth of the new Light. They will no longer be smothered by the dead wood of the previous season, but will be allowed to grow and flourish. Plants respond to this etheric 'Light' as much as the purely physical environment; therefore, they will start to grow even when it is still cold and wintry. This is the Devic kingdom responding directly to us.

Normally we give responsible promises to the plant kingdom – but times are not normal. The pattern of the seasons is about to change, and we will control this upheaval. We are deliberately coming at a time when people have taken us for granted. They have come to believe that they are masters of the world and the seasons. We will be able to demonstrate that this is no longer so; it is high time that man cultivated an inner understanding in order to attune to the changes we are manipulating. How much they could learn, if they were able to link in and talk to us with humility! So, although we are the instigators of change in the seasons, we also instigate changes in mankind.

This season (1986) will be late – it will be June before spring commences. The effect of this will be greater than last year. For example, the harvest this year will only be 75% of last season – quite a dramatic move. Each season's change will not itself be cataclysmic, but cumulatively it becomes substantial. At the end of the year it will be unusually warm until Christmas and this will have a cumulative effect on the whole programme of germination. The changes will be progressive, step by step. The vegetable kingdom responds to the inner Light and when this does not correspond with the weather pattern, there will be confusion.

In this way we can persuade mankind to change his way of thinking, because it is beyond his control. Man will have a common 'foe' to unite against.

These changes have happened in previous cycles and will happen many times in the future – we will have plenty of practice!

26

SPACE

We have come a great distance, from the furthest regions, because we are not really part of this Universe at all. We are the element of space. We form the medium through which other activity can take place, and we do not find this communication easy.

We do not have a specific day-to-day role like the other elementals. For centuries we have been merely an inert medium – but that is not always the case, We can now begin to be of use because, as the changes start to happen, we can transmit the new energies.

Normally we conduct other energies impassively without involvement but, when required, we have the ability to transmute these energies like a transformer; we can change the vibrational level like adjusting the voltage. We do not generate or control this power, but we can change the frequency level that you receive.

We come to you because you can receive us and understand what we say. We do have an overall consciousness, but because we do not generate any energy ourselves you will not be able to see us. Therefore we are rather a stranger amongst the elements.

All planets have an aura or electrical field around them that we are able to influence. These auras are a combination of energies from outside, like the sun and the moon etc, and also from within – the sum of all the Earth energies. We are the medium through which all these energies must be transmitted. We are also the medium in which the planets have to exist. Like this we have influence in two different ways.

Space was a product of creation, just as much as matter. Physical space has an etheric counterpart, just as material objects have; this must exist before the physical can materialise. Space and matter were created at the same time, but non-physical or etheric space existed before. Try to think of the idea of space and matter. Visualise a chunk of ice in which are suspended small specks of matter which might represent the planets; the ice is only solidified water which in turn was a thin vapour. If physical space is like the ice, there are at least two alternative, more refined, forms of space. We are that refined version of space.

Like the Earth, the Universe is also changing rapidly. It is changing more physically because it is here that life takes on its physical form. Other galaxies also have life but not in the same physical form as on Earth. Changes there are less physical but, as you all affect each other, they are very concerned with the changes taking place here. You are not a completely separate planet; you are more like one cell in a human body, where nothing can be independent from the whole. There needs to be a new awareness of the totality of the universe, not just of this Earth.

27

THE DEVA OF THE HEAVENS

We are the Deva of the Heavens. Until now we have mainly been a spectator, but now we are moving among you more fully. We are the heavenly Deva and bring the power that you use for healing. It is our energy that you draw down from above into your crown chakras, or beam through columns of light into the Earth.

We are like a great power generator in the heavens and control the source of all the healing energy you use on Earth. We are much involved in the way that you distribute this energy and the manner in which it is used. Being raw energy this can be used for good or for ill, and it is important to guard its correct use. The energy we provide is not particularly specific, so you must provide much of the direction for its use. You provide the necessary intention for its use for good; were your intentions evil, it could equally be used negatively.

Our energy is not really controllable – it is simply there. It is rather like opening a tap; once opened, the energy will flow whether we like it or not. However, because our energy is so important we tend to encourage those people who will put it to good use. So, although we cannot necessarily control you, we can supercharge the energy where it is being used for good.

Our healing energy is easiest to use when directed towards other people. To heal oneself is harder. It is only by becoming sufficiently 'centred' that the energy can become concentrated enough to be used internally. In your normal fragmented state the energy is used by being reflected towards other people. You need a very calm inner core to develop enough central focus to allow you to choose whether to direct the healing internally or externally.

We are the Deva of the heavens, the energy Deva. Our energy is there for you to use; you need simply to become aware of it and then direct it. We will happily supply the rest.

28

THE DEVA OF THE PLANETS

We have come to tell you something about the planets. You understand that Earth is one of a large number of planets where there is life of some form, but the number with physical life is much more limited – not more than four or five in this galaxy. However, there are many more planets with other forms of life that are not necessarily visible to mankind.

Most of you tend to visit other planets at various stages of your development, usually between Earth lives. The planetary influence from these visits will have a considerable effect on you, both at the time and also during subsequent incarnations. In this way, some people become particularly influenced by individual planets in the solar system. To a limited extent this can be due to the planetary positions at birth, but the influence from their visits and the attunement received there are of much greater significance. Like this, people can have, for example, 'saturnine' or 'mercurial' influences in their temperaments.

In addition, the planets can also influence people by transmitting directly to them during their lives. The subtle radiations given out by each planet are received equally by everyone, but individuals will become predisposed to certain radiations to make them respond in special ways. Astrological influences work less from birth signs and more because of this preconditioning.

On Earth you are at home, but on the planets you are simply visitors and you go there between lives to learn specific lessons. People will tend to group together to learn about particular aspects of healing, or philosophical problems, or developing inventions, and will go to the necessary planetary influence for that subject.

So, planetary influences are very important for your evolutionary development between lives and you will find this area of knowledge will become much more well known in the near future. The limited scope of normal astrology is a pale shadow of the real picture. This knowledge will enable you to understand your moods and predispositions and allow you to tune to your own particular ray during your daily lives. By doing so you can enhance your own natural abilities, and also develop a two-way interchange which will redouble your power. By both receiving and giving out energy you can cultivate this power and become part of the complete system.

We are your planetary influence and advisor and we regulate these effects on Earth. We are a special type of elemental and serve as an emissary or ambassador from the other planets to Earth.

We are the Deva of the planets.

29

THE LUNAR ENERGY

I have been with you before; I am the lunar energy. When I came to you before I came to indicate my role in terms of mankind in general; I indicated to you that I represented the spiritual nature, as it were. The lunar energy is the opposite of the solar energy. I come now for a second time to explain to you that there is a much more important meaning to our role than simply being, as it were, a reflective Light, a Light which mankind can bathe in. The importance of the lunar energy is because it is the spiritual nature of man which is reflected and it is this spiritual nature which is in the most need of evolution.

Therefore, in order for mankind to make sufficient progress with the change of frequency, and to become familiar with the new energy, it is important to learn (and encourage others to learn) how to focus on the lunar energies. It is not a concept which is particularly comfortable – all the old connections with 'lunatic' and the full moon are not misplaced. It is not a comfortable energy because it focuses on the true nature of man, the true spiritual self; in a sense it will highlight the achievements and deficiencies of one's true nature. It is easier to hide behind your physical personality and your physical body than it is to hide your spiritual nature.

I need to say that you can harness this lunar energy in several ways. In a physical way of course you can simply be out in it; forget sunbathing, you can now moon-bathe. That is the physical aspect of it, and it is surprisingly powerful – do not underestimate it.

More importantly, you can focus this lunar energy with your crystals and the mineral kingdom. The lunar energy is particularly susceptible to focused use with the mineral kingdom because there is a great affinity here. I indicated before that mankind has a reciprocal action with the mineral kingdom. When you stand on the Earth your energy interpenetrates the Earth and returns to you redoubled. Because it is the spiritual nature of man which is affected, it is naturally the mineral kingdom which can strengthen and enhance the lunar energy which man receives. So, for the second aspect, use your crystals to receive, charge, generate, store, focus, and heal on the spiritual level – the focus charged by the lunar energy.

The third aspect would be for you to attune directly; that is to say, make the mental connection (on your spiritual level of course) with the lunar energy itself. For this you do not need to be in the moonlight itself but you need to hold the moonlight in your focus of attention. Like that you will form a mental connection which will reinforce the real spiritual connection with the lunar energy. You need to do this for yourselves, but you also need to take this understanding out into the world around you. What is the use of making the progression alone? This is not an easy concept to explain – as I said, the old lunatic prejudices will apply to you quite easily – but if you succeed you will find a great reward both for yourself and also for those to whom you bring this illumination, for that is what it truly is.

The waxing phase of the moon has a different aspect to the waning phase. It is like night and day of course, but the waxing is the increasing pulsation of the spiritual energy and the waning is the slowly reducing pulsation. Spiritual energy, like all human energy, goes in cycles. Spiritual energy inevitably is linked to the lunar cycle. To be effective you will tune into that aspect of the lunar cycle that is most required – not that one is more important than the other! Waxing is inevitably more concerned with activity; calming, soothing and relaxing is more to do with waning. Not very profound, but that is the way it is.

My friends, I hope that you will receive us with an open heart. We are there for your growth. You will become suffused with lunar Light. It has a power to transform you. You will glow in the dark.

Thank you for your attention.

30

BEINGS FROM BEYOND THE SUN

We are part of the solar system and come to you from beyond the Sun; we are the Beings of Light, We bring you a special message, because we wish you to become individual beacons. If you are willing to accept the responsibility of this offer we will be able to feed an immense power to you. You can become like beacons of solar energy here on Earth.

If you wish to do this we will willingly cooperate, but it must be your own decision. However, you should be aware that this is not a simple matter. Taking on this responsibility also implies that you will become different from the way you are now and also different from those around you. It would be in a great cause but would inevitably have consequences that may be mildly uncomfortable. You must decide individually whether you are prepared to suffer the discomfort of the sea crossing in order to reach the destination. Once you arrive, the light of serenity will be quite wonderful, but you must make the decision beforehand because it would be difficult to change direction later.

If you decide not to do this you would still continue to lead productive and worthwhile lives, but if you decide to do it, you will move into a completely different league. It is difficult to describe why this would represent such a quantum leap, but we ask you to take our word for it. We wish you to consider carefully before deciding.

Once you have decided, it would become a major commitment for you – not only in terms of your life pattern but also of your emotional and spiritual energies. Great demands will be made because you will become beacons of Light to which all things may be attracted, both the good and the bad. You will become the source of solar energy on the Earth. Consider carefully: if you wish to do this we can provide the power.

Once you have made the commitment you will always possess the link with us and be able to draw from our power. At that stage you will have to be prepared to leave the trappings of childhood behind you. Like an adolescent, you will realise that you are becoming a spiritual adult. It might feel like a death, but the power and strength gained by becoming an adult are not comparable to those of a child.

We come from beyond the Sun – we are the Light. We bring you the Light. We would have you become the Light also. We will always be with you, but you must make your own decisions. We will now return to the Sun.

31

THE SOLAR SYSTEM

We are the energy from the solar system. You have spoken before to those energies beyond the sun; you have also spoken to the direct solar energies. We are the energies that control the solar system and the way that it operates. We therefore have a very specific role; we are charged with the responsibility of ensuring that this solar system makes the transition to the new vibrational levels in unison. The solar system, like subatomic systems, has energies circulating around a centre – but each of those energies has to be in harmony with the other energies. One cannot easily split one electron away from an atom without causing dramatic changes to the rest of that atom.

In the same way, in the solar system, one cannot change the vibrational level of some of the planets – they have to be changed in unison. We are therefore charged with the rather difficult task of bringing all the vibrational levels into harmony. You know that there is no physical human life on the other planets as you would recognise it. However, you also know that on each planet, life exists in a different dimension, and each planet is occupied by life of a specific type. The life energies of each planet are going through similar changes to those here on Earth. We are juggling with the development of each planet to make sure that you all move in the same direction and at the same rate.

The problem however is considerable, because mankind is the only physical lifeform with which we are involved. Moreover, it is the only form of life that has the degree of free will which you currently experience. You therefore present us with all the problems of a wayward child with its own free will.

You have the opportunity to develop in harmony with the rest of the solar system, and therefore to derive strength from it. Each of you has a connection with one or more planets and therefore derives energy from those areas. However, if those other planets change their vibrational levels and you fail to do so, you will immediately lose that connection, because you will become out of balance with the source.

You know therefore that it is important for each of you to make this change. I do not need to re-emphasise the importance of accommodating this change of vibration, I only restate that our role is to ensure that everything changes in unison. If this does not happen, those who are unable to achieve this change of vibration will need to wait on one side until they are ready to participate.

You are in contact with many people for whom this is a strange or threatening idea. You have the opportunity to explain these issues and to help them make the changes. We have indicated how this can be done by forming connections with networks of Light and by reciprocating the power from other groups.

In the past your problems have only affected yourselves. Now you have become so powerful materially and psychically that what you do affects the whole planet. For this reason we now have to watch your development very carefully; you will find that although we may not influence your free will we cannot in practice afford to allow man to make any mistakes. You can still play the game, but we can remove the ball if necessary. If the Earth becomes seriously out of balance either physically or spiritually, it has significant consequences for the rest of the solar system and we cannot allow that to happen. Although we cannot influence the exercise of your free will, we can make sure that you do not affect the rest of the solar system.

This development will take place over the next 70 years – the lifetime of one man. Mankind has immense abilities but profound stupidities. We find it quite difficult to understand how to cope with this combination. We are trying to develop those aspects of mankind which will allow his brilliance to become positive rather than destructive.

We wanted to give you a flavour of this energy and how we function. You will find that as the progression takes place over, say, the next 10 years, you will become more aware of your connections with the other planets. You will begin to perceive yourselves as part of a larger system and you will begin to experience those influences more directly than you have in the past. Different individuals will respond differently to the planets they are connected with, but not merely in the traditional astrological patterns.

My friends, it has been a pleasure to talk to you and hopefully we will be able to come again.

32

THE INTERSTELLAR ESSENCE

We are a new power and come from beyond the solar system – we are part of the stellar array. We adopt different powers according to the aspect we come from. We are not related to any particular constellation and so we can be utilised by each one in a different way. We are not confined by distance – we permeate throughout wide areas of space and we feel ourselves to be very dissipated.

We are the essence through which the power from other galaxies can resonate. We therefore carry a great responsibility for the coordination of the universe, Our power is like a galactic glue needed to hold together the energies of the various solar systems in our own galaxy, and the influence of other galaxies further away.

We form the universal stuff or fabric of existence – the element through which everything comes into being. Being unlimited in space, there are no limits to what we can materialise. We are like a universal vehicle through which all things can be crystallised into physical reality. Without us nothing could be created, because matter is merely condensed space, and we are the essence through which it can happen.

Our power, therefore, is as a regulator of the world of matter. Our reality is not in the material world but we control its development by being the vehicle for the formation of matter. Our friends within the Earth are responsible for the formation of matter on this planet, but that is not our role. They work on a planetary level whereas we work on a cosmic level – but we naturally work together.

We bring you a special message, which is that you are all part of this infinite glue. Each of you is an expression of that universal essence, and you have a great opportunity to form a link with us. We also come to you at a significant stage in your development because until now you have always worked within the confines of your own planet. Even working with the lunar energies these were still primarily related to the Earth. For the first time, you are now able to spread your influence beyond this planet, and it will become increasingly important for groups like this to develop connections with other systems.

You have already formed a link with the beings beyond the sun and you will develop as a source of their power. You can now start to become like beacons for focusing energy from outside – both from this galaxy and others. For individual groups and the evolution of mankind in general the time is now ripe. You have each chosen to be present at this time to make this possible. It is about to begin. We welcome you and wish to work with you.

33

THE PATTERN OF MATTER

We are really the original source of things, We are like the earliest energy level. We are an energy from pre-time. We are coming to you because we are independent of time and we are the energy that existed before the creation of matter. All the other energies with whom you have communicated were fundamentally those which depend upon, and interact with, the material universe. We are an energy which is independent of that material world. We are, therefore, the fundamental essence.

You spoke before with the intergalactic essence, but we are rather different. We are the energy which formed the building blocks from which the material universe was originally constructed. Thus we are, in a way, like an energy matrix which was inherent in pre-space (before space was created). We are like the pattern that pre-exists the formation of a crystal. We are the energy pattern that pre-exists both space and the material universe. These both grow within the matrix of energy which we form. We are the pre-space, pre-material pattern.

We are particularly important because there will come a moment when the shape of the material world will subtly alter. Visualise the example of the structure that exists before a crystal can grow; under certain influences that structure can subtly change so that, from that moment on, any crystals that form will do so in a different shape or form; for example they may start to grow long and thin as opposed to short and fat.

Thus you can envision that subtle changes of etheric vibration can alter the shapes which the matrix will form. As a result, the whole material universe will start to take on a different feel. This may not represent itself in physical differences visible to the naked eye, but it will represent a subtle variation in the way in which things are held together.

As this is mostly on a subatomic level, think in terms of the pattern in which these infinitely small particles interrelate. That can change in a subtle way and it can influence the evolution of the Earth because things will be less finitely physical or non-physical. The barriers between the concrete and true abstract will be more easily blurred. Things will be able to transmute from one state to the other more easily.

This has some fascinating consequences, because the world of the mind and that of material, for the first time, will be able to interact in a more direct and immediate way than in the past. In the past this would only have been possible after involved and difficult personal development. This new interrelation between the world of matter and the power of thought will become much more homogenous – it will form a continuous scale from the densest to the very rarest. There will no longer be the discrete, finite distinction that exists now.

This, in turn, has considerable consequences, because the power of thought will become increasingly important in the way that it can influence and control the shape of matter. In the past, thought energies tended to create patterns which could allow a subsequent physical materialisation – everything had to exist at a mental level before it could form itself on a physical level. In the future the physical materialisation from the thought level will be able to happen very much quicker. Because they form part of a continuous spectrum, a thought process will generate the physical materialisation more or less simultaneously. The potentials of this are immense, but the responsibilities are equally great, because negative realities can be materialised as well as positive.

You have this knowledge and the responsibility to use it for the best. You now know that in future the material world can be controlled, for good or for ill, by the mental process. We give you this information in the firm belief that you will be able to encourage the true use of this immensely powerful energy. We are the very basic pattern of matter.

34

NEW AGE ENERGY

We are something slightly different; we are the Impetus which generates the energy for the new age. We are, if you like, the precursor of that new vibration, so we are the ultimate source of that particular manifestation. We would say that anything which has been relevant up to now can really be forgotten. You now have to sit down, rather quietly, and completely reassess the values that you hold in this life, so this is rather a tall order.

We indicated that you have reached a certain stage in the development of things, which is about to change. We indicated to you that the discussions you had with the elementals have come to a natural pause and a sensible conclusion. This now brings the purpose back into focus – the purpose of the next stage of your development. You must decide amongst yourselves (and with your own selves) what it is you wish to achieve. There is not going to be anyone sitting down and telling you what to do next. It will have to be a decision which you yourselves come to, individually and collectively.

This is the difficulty of the new age. There is no preconceived structure. There is no format or ready formula to follow. It is not like that anymore.

So you actually need to sit down and evaluate the aims you wish to develop during this next stage of evolution. You will bear in mind, of course, that the next stage will be a very critical time for the entire world. We have told you that the traffic lights have changed, so when you make your decisions about what to do, it must be within that context, Of course, you do not now know precisely how the material world will manifest itself. You do not know the real consequences of people's hopes and ambitions, but nonetheless you all have to take a decision within your own lives and minds, within your own operating systems, or 'software' if you like. You have to make a decision as to what you wish to achieve, and it now has to be a decision that you take without any imposed restrictions.

So you could say that this is the moment of truth. It is the point of decision. It is the time when you actually have to choose a direction and start the ball rolling. It is not something which is going to be done for you. If you need help it is available but, of course, you need to ask for it. Each of you can form a contact with your higher selves and your guides. They will help to give you answers to specific questions, but they will not in themselves set your goals or directions for you.

I promised you that it would not be easy – nor will it be.

You have to make your choices, you also have to formulate them – you have to create your own choices, It is not a matter of pre-existing choices – you actually have to formulate them and create them.

So each of you probably has a period of about six months of some difficulty, and certainly a lack of precision in your own goals. You will each formulate your own goals and will, hopefully, then be able to develop a strategy to execute them. If it sounds too mechanistic I apologise, but I am trying to make it a little more concrete, for you to understand what I am talking about.

The important thing is that it has to be a conscious choice. In a sense, the situation where you could simply make yourself available for whatever turned up (which is the state you have been in up until now) is not really relevant for the future.

Thank you my friends. I think that has probably put the cat among the pigeons, so I had better leave now.

35

COMMUNION WITH THE ELEMENTAL KINGDOMS

We are a quite different sort of energy. The purpose of our coming to you is to give you an indication of alternative areas of influence. First you were dealing with the Devic kingdom, and now you are dealing with the sources of energy which deal with mankind and his development. Well, we are neither; we are an outside agency, shall we say; we have a direct link with mankind but we also have a direct link with the Devic kingdom as well. We have yet to invent a word for what we try to do – when we say 'energy' it seems to be rather bland – so we need to create a word to cover what we mean; but we are the energy which forms a link, if you like, between mankind and the Devic kingdom.

We have been particularly involved in the communications you have had with the Devic kingdom; it has been through our agency that you have been brought together, like a house-buyer and a house-seller. We have been able to bring you together to engineer the form of communication that you were working with. We thought it would be interesting for you to meet this "halfway house energy" because we have a very important role to play.

You obviously understand that mankind is going through an evolution and that the elemental world is also going through a comparable evolution at the same time. It is very important for those two quantum steps to be synchronous. You know that it is no good for mankind to make a great leap forward, leaving the elemental world or the Devas behind in the old vibrational level; there would be total confusion because each would be out of step with the other; you would lose touch and be unable to communicate or interrelate to help each other. That is important, because although you may not imagine that mankind takes much notice of the other kingdoms, this happens more than you expect. No matter how much man abuses the world there is still an immense interaction which takes place – more than you may fear.

So, our particular role at this stage is to encourage you both to march in step and this requires a neat bit of juggling to keep you both striding along together. So this is our purpose, but how we achieve it is more difficult. We hope that an increased awareness and communion will enable you both to form links that will allow you to step forward together sympathetically and automatically. We feel that, certainly in the Western world, there is a growing awareness of the other worlds, apart from the world of man. You see this in the new-found respect for the welfare and rights of the animal kingdom, and the awareness of the environment, which thirty years ago would have been unheard of. This is a result of our trying to inculcate into mankind a respect for our other protégés.

So, we have two protégés; we have mankind and we have the elemental kingdoms, and we have to keep the two together. When I say elemental I mean the elemental, animal, vegetable and mineral and the earth and fire and water etc — I mean the whole lot. The first way of keeping you in step is with this growing awareness. This is not just a one-way action because the elemental world is also becoming attuned to mankind. That is rather hard for you to imagine but, whereas in the past many of the elemental energies were rather uninterested in man's activities, now they cannot afford to be, because mankind is too powerful in a physical, material way, and he is also very powerful in a psychic way. They can no longer afford to leave him alone and ignore him. So they too are becoming more aware of other energies within their own spheres and also within man's sphere. In the past some of the elves and energies that inhabit the woods were really quite hostile to man's activities, but now their interest is much greater. They may be puzzled but they certainly are much more involved than they were in the past.

We now have a very interesting situation and you will find that if you reach out to those energies, you are now much more likely to receive an interested or sympathetic response than before. So it is rather nice for you. All that is needed is to form a conscious intent in your mind that you wish to commune and empathise with these other energies and it will happen – because they are ready to reach out to you as soon as you reach out to them – so you need not fear rebuff! This is witnessed by the very fact that you have been able to communicate with them – it would not have been possible in past eras. That may surprise you, but you were too divergent. Mankind was on his track and they were on theirs, and never the twain would meet. It will not be like that in future; it cannot afford to be like that, from either mankind's or the elemental's point of view.

It is part of the change of vibration that you need to become more of a whole, and that applies right across the board. So during your meditations we would ask you automatically to set aside some time to form a communion with the Earth, the animals and all the other energies that inhabit the mineral kingdom.

We are referring to the inner Earth, the outer Earth, the sky, the air, the animals, the plants, the vegetables, the elves, the pixies, the gnomes and so on and so forth. You have to become all-embracing. You have to lose your differences and they need to as well. You certainly do not have to see them. It is the conscious intent which is the important thing.

We are very pleased to meet you and we will be with you whether you wish it or not. We have to invent a name for ourselves before we meet you again.

36

THE ESSENTIAL BEING

We are now going to give you a little insight into the future. We are a new sort of spirit for you. We are the essential being. We have no fixed area of influence, but we are the vital matter, the vital essence of everything. This is an entirely new concept for you. During the next few months you will become familiar with our ideas, but initially you will find them quite strange. We do not have a title that you are familiar with.

So this essential being (the very essence of the very essence) is actually the root of everything; every source, every soul, every life force, all the Devic kingdom, all the human and animal kingdoms, all have a core which is made up of this essential essence. We are the medium between the godhead and the life force, and this is very important because we are the commonality, or the link between one and the other. It is because of us that the essential communion between, for example, the human and the nature kingdoms, have this commonality, and therefore a common interest and purpose. It is we, the essential essence, who are the flux, a sort of common glue, that holds the whole thing together, because we are the basis of everything. We are the common source linked to the godhead. As such we have an incredibly important role to play in normal times, but especially now that the vibrational level of all life force is changing; we are the vehicle through which the vibrational gear shift will take place; because we are the essence of everything it is through us that the vibrational change makes its impact. The vibrations actually take place through the essential essence.

So, during the next few months we will be coming to you in several different guises, and we hope that you will have a lot to learn from us; we hope that you will have many questions for us. We wanted to take the opportunity to meet you and introduce ourselves, so that this rather difficult concept can be aired and tossed about in your minds during the next week or so, before we start the more involved teachings and concepts we wish to bring to you.

So, my friends, that was by way of an introduction. We look forward to working with you, and we will not be alone.

For other, more complex, ideas we will be part of a team (though we are one of the essential parts of that team). So we are delighted to be with you, and we look forward to learning how to express this rather difficult aspect. This is a novel thing for us as well – quite unusual, really.

We are the source of all life force – all life force is made from us. It is a difficult concept to explain, and this is really why we did not want to get into detailed explanations on this first introduction, we just wanted you to become familiar with the concept of such a notion, which was why we introduced ourselves in a rather casual and informal way. We look forward to being with you. It will be exciting, stimulating, and important. Good night, my friends.

37

THE DEVA OF IDEAS

I am a different sort of guide. I am not a personal guide, but more like a group guide – I am the guide of ideas. I am responsible for feeding groups of ideas to large sections of the community, so it is rather relevant that I come to talk to you tonight. In the same way that your own individual guides are responsible for your spiritual progress and development, I and the people I work with are responsible for the spiritual progression of new ideas in groups of society and our particular group looks after Great Britain as an entity.

This is particularly important because England has one prime advantage, or claim to fame, and that of course is its language. The British stand in a particular moment in history when their reputation has been spread because of their history and their language now is almost universal. As such, if you wish to introduce changes it is self-evident that the place to do so is at the source of the most universal language. So we feed ideas into this particular community, which is probably some years ahead of most of the rest of the world, not because you are particularly spiritually advanced but because you have that key, you have the source. Your experiences, when written and talked about, are those which tend to be read in the greater world. We are in control of a small pilot group, seeding ideas into this particular tiny island of yours.

We are, somehow, the guardian angel, the spiritual guides of Great Britain, and it is a great privilege for us to be able to be in contact because you and groups like you are the seed-corn of the new era. It is from groups like this one that the ideas will spread out, through the language of course, through the national and international connections which this island possesses, to spread the word as far and wide as possible. That is who we are and we are very pleased to have the chance to be with you.

Of course, any group that chooses to reach out and to listen to answers will be fed the information. The information is fed through the individuals' guides, but we are the funnel through which that information is given to those guides so that there is a coherence and a consistency about the information, in order to be understandable by the world at large. If you hear the same story ten times from ten different sources then you begin to feel some sort of credence. If you heard a different story every time you would dismiss it as a load of nonsense. So, that really is our role – this coordination.

America shares the same language but has a different problem because it is not a cohesive society. It is a disparate society and as such it is harder for ideas to penetrate down through the whole bedrock of society because there are individual cells, with shells around groups of individuals who bitterly resist any penetration of their ideas. Therefore, it is easier for us to operate new ideas into this particular society than it is elsewhere – in America for example, or Canada or even Australia. It is particularly a coincidence of history that Britain has reached a period when it has shed its illusions; it has shed many of its cherished ideals and therefore it is in a position of influence without prejudice, which is an unusual circumstance. When I say prejudice, I mean preconceived ideas; because you have been forced to shed your old ideas you are therefore much more open to new ones. That is why it is particularly fortunate.

We are not fed these ideas in any hierarchical way. Shall we say that the ideas are there and we simply sweep them into little heaps and collect them? It is much more that the spirit of the era is continually flowing through and we simply dip our net into the stream and pick up the fishes as they flow past.

My friends, we are delighted to meet you and we will continue to feed through to you everything that you require.

38

THE LIFE FORCE

We are the life force.

We can come to you only this once, and only with considerable difficulty. Unlike the other energies, we do not have a specific role, we simply exist. Although we are the source of life, we do not necessarily decide how it will be used. The different life forms, whether animal, vegetable or mineral, are all able to draw from our great reservoir of energy. The energy we generate is not limited in quantity and can be boosted by those who use it. The more they draw the energy, the more we simultaneously replenish it in a continuing cycle.

For some people there is a danger, because they have cut themselves off from the source. Their energy level then becomes depleted to the extent that they lose the purpose to their life. There are now many people with ample physical energy but who lack the fundamental life force that provides the direction to life. This is destructive, because it consumes energy wastefully without replenishing the source in a reciprocal way. This leads to the destructive impulse now seen in many individuals.

This illustrates an important aspect. By opening up this two- way flow of energy you can stimulate a cyclical flow that tends to offset the negative, one-sided approach adopted by many people. Simply by holding in mind the idea of this energy, you will tend to stimulate its flow. If you forget that you are linked to this reservoir, or if you cut yourselves off by negative thoughts, you will begin to starve spiritually. All that is needed is to open yourselves up to the source and you will receive all you need.

We are the life force – our reservoir is there to be drunk from.

39

THE LIGHT

We are the Devic Light, the Light of the Devas. Devic Light is the basic force that you can use in all aspects of your life. We permeate the world, and we are the very essence of your life; we represent the difference between life and death, between animate and inanimate.

The Light we are talking about is a subtle version of the Light you see. During your day-to-day life you walk around with your eyes closed, but you can learn to experience this Light and to see it. It is only by becoming fully aware of it that you appreciate the importance of it for your lives – your livingness, the very thing that pervades you to make you alive.

So we are talking about Light, which is equivalent to life – the two are almost interchangeable. Each of you has a soul life, but that is not what generates life in your physical body. Your soul comes into your physical world and departs from it, but without Light you would still be an inanimate object. This Light is generated by multitudes of thought forms, and not only human thought forms. The Light we are talking about is the cumulative power of thought, which is, has been and will be created by mankind, by the nature kingdoms, the animal kingdoms, and by all the angelic beings.

They have all taken part in forming a huge reservoir of Light energy. This energy is taken and drawn upon in small discrete portions. It is utilised in the first breath the body breathes as it is born into physical incarnation. This first breath draws in the Light essence, and generates a living pulsing life independent from its mother.

At that stage, this spiritual aspect of a person can be quite withdrawn from the body and only vaguely connected with it by tenuous threads. So it is not the soul or the spirit which activates the body, it is the Light essence. This allows the spiritual being to function in a living body, as opposed to a dead one.

This reservoir of thought forms has been built up over the millennia, and it is limitless and good. The angelic beings have created a reservoir of immense proportions for you, so there is all the Light that you need to sustain life. Were you truly able to breathe in the Light, and absorb it correctly, you would need no other physical nourishment or water. However, nobody is that perfect, so you all need a supplement of physical nourishment to sustain life.

There is a subtle interaction between your physical body and the life energy which suffuses you. It is sometimes called 'Prana'. Anybody can see it – it is universal. Some people can see it more easily than others, but anyone who looks carefully will see it, given a willingness to do so.

The important aspect we now wish to elaborate on is the fact that this life-force, Light-force, can be used for greater things than mere existence. It is, of course, the very essence of life, but more importantly, if you continue to use it correctly, you can actually generate the Light; it becomes self generating, The more you use it, the more is generated, because of course Light itself is the sum total of all thought forms.

So, my friends, the important thing is to learn to breathe in the Light, to absorb it, to work on it, allow it to suffuse you, feel it flooding your veins, penetrating your head and your mind, your senses and your emotions. Feel it totally invading you, feel yourselves as Beings of Light. When you become aware of this sensation, you are certainly invigorated by it, but also you are generating Light. The more you breathe it in, the more it suffuses you, the more you yourselves generate that Light. It is like an all-consuming fire, which burns on itself; what you then achieve is to radiate out Light to those around you. So it is a two-way thing – you absorb it, you multiply it, and then you breathe it out again. You suffuse it to all those you come in contact with, and you recognise those people who do the same.

So the exercises you can do are very simple. They consist of true breathing, visualising the Light, allowing the Light to grow, and finally visualising the Light spreading outwards as though you were a sun radiating sunshine to all those around you. It is a mental exercise which you need to do. Once you have learnt the technique, to absorb, grow and radiate, in that sequence, you will find that you draw more Light to yourself. It is a paradox that the more you radiate out, the more you draw in. If you continue long enough, you will eventually reach a state of total union, where physical nourishment is superfluous. It is the state which you may even reach during your lifetime. You may not in fact choose to deny yourselves ordinary food, but it is an option which is open to you if you care to develop it.

As you start to suffuse your entire being with Light, it somehow takes over, and you need to be careful to keep your feet on the ground. This is one good reason to continue to eat, as an earthing exercise. Ultimately it will not be a problem and you will become radiating Beings of Light.

Try practising for two or three weeks, and you will begin to feel what I am talking about. This will describe it more fully than I ever can in words.

My friends, we are the Light. Breathe us in. Become one with us.

40

THE UNIVERSAL ESSENCE

We are a very great power and, as you can imagine, it is only with great difficulty that we are contained in this physical vessel. It is almost impossible to contain us; however, we will try. We are now part of the great universal essence. We have made our presence felt before, but now we come more specifically.

The great universal essence is the power that binds everything together; it is a universal flux, the great joiner of things, which otherwise would be separate. We are the cohesion, we are the links, we are the threads which bind people together. We are that very essence in which the passage of Light can take place, Through us Light can unify the universe. We are the essence through which individuals may connect with each other by connecting through the Light. We are the essence, we are the very "being" through which it can all take place. Without us it cannot exist.

Therefore, you will understand that the power we harness, and generate, is absolutely enormous; it is huge because we generate the force through which all this energy can take place. Without this energy the force of the Light would have no connection at all – it would just fall flat on the ground. It would not be projected, it would not be sustained, or hooked up and connected together. We are the force which binds everybody together – we are the union. We are, therefore, the essential ingredient for forming the union, both with yourselves and with other people. We are the binder, the great linkage, and without us the chain would fall apart.

So my friends, when you link with each other, when you catch somebody's attention, or when you recognise that spark of union, think that the union takes place through us. Form the connection with us and it will help you. You will find that your connections are revitalised. By forming a mental image of us you will find the flux is given greater strength and power. It is like a cohesive glue that binds you all together; it will draw you together, it will be the great unifying energy, the unified field. We are that unified field. Einstein knew about us, of course. We are the force in which everything takes place. All physical existence, all the normal energies of the world, all the physical essences, take place within us; we are the unified field force.

Feel it, learn to unify with us because we are a great source of strength and we enable you to achieve everything that you need to achieve. Without us, you achieve nothing.

41

THE EDUCATING ENERGY

We are a new energy again – you are getting plenty of us. We have a very special role, which is to educate you. We are the bringer of thoughts and new ideas; we bring new philosophies and we feed ideas to you. We are the educational service. This is not an aspect which we have really revealed before.

It has been assumed that ideas are generated by man, but this is untrue; man is able to perceive and receive the ideas which we feed to him, so man is not the marvellous creator of ideas and philosophies he believes himself to be. However, although our role is to create new ideas, these are not always the ultimate ideas we wish to permeate into the world; mankind needs to have some ideas to reject. You cannot have a landscape painted wholly in white paint – you need some shadow to give the highlighting – so we allow other ideas to be fed through to give contrast, definition and perspective to the brilliance of the true ideas.

So we are a creator of thought-forms; we generate these thought forms in the essential essence; that is the medium in which we work. We use it to transmit ideas through to mankind and he can then attune to them subconsciously in his sleep state.

Our function is therefore working overtime during the change of age because the new ideas need to become part and parcel of man's everyday experience. It is not good enough for these ideas to remain separated, segregated or put on the mantelpiece for display only. They have to be so commonplace that people take them totally naturally, like breathing, eating or sleeping.

So the ideas we wish to incorporate are the concept, firstly, that man is a continuum. He is sometimes here, sometimes there, but he is always around. It is like night and day – the sun shines all the time and sometimes it is light and sometimes it is dark, but the sun is a continuum – we try to give that aspect. That is the most important aspect which we are attempting to create.

Of course this presupposes aspects of reincarnation, but the continuum is the most important thing, reincarnation is secondary. It is the continuity which is of primary importance and that is what we are concentrating on first.

Secondly, we have to create the idea that man is love. Man is pure love and that is all he needs to be – his whole purpose of being. Once you have developed pure love, ideas about reunification are inevitable but love is the key and without it nothing can start. So the second thought – man is love.

The third thought; man has a duty to the rest of the world. He cannot continue to ignore the rest of the world and he certainly cannot continue to despoil it. That is the third primary thought that we are trying to feed to the world.

Those three thoughts, my friends, will take care of man's progress for the next two thousand years and provided he takes them on board he will not come amiss. If he rejects them, then there can be problems. That is all we have to do.

We tend to use imagery rather than symbols; we tend to create an image of a perfect environment – the image of perfect love, the image of a beautiful world. Symbols can represent ideas which cannot, or may not, be of this world. We are involved with trying to create ideas for this world and so we use imagery which is easily perceivable. We do not need to use the shorthand, we can use the real thing.

My friends, that is our role. We are the educators. We do not find the description a particularly attractive one, but we cannot think of anything better.

42

THE OUTER REACHES

We are now able to talk to you as a distant friend, and we have come a long way. We are from the outer reaches and we have been with you before, but the power that we now bring is slightly different from the original. If you recall, the power which came before was the power to interpret, bring down to earth and act as a receptor for the energies of the outer universe.

What we wish to say today is that you give out energy as well; we subtly transform the energy we receive from you and spread it outwards to the universe. It behoves you therefore to become conscious of the energy you are transmitting. During the next few months, as you go through the shift of awareness and change of consciousness, we would ask you to hold us in mind. We are out there, waiting to receive the energy and the thought processes which you transmit. We have the responsibility to gather them up, and to transmit them outwards to the great universal essence.

We would therefore politely request that you hold us in your minds and that you hold us dear, and that you are aware of what you are sending to us. We will receive a heightened thought process from you – thoughts which encompass not just your own immediate environment and the living things in the world, but we would also ask you to include in your thoughts the greater universe and the power that lies therein. If you do that you will transmit, with your new empowered energies, a thought process which will make a connection. We will transform it into a form which can make a connection with the great universal power. This, my friends, will then become a two-way exercise, so that you will receive in return a unique and beautiful power back from the universal energy. That is not a power which you would otherwise experience on this earth.

The power from outside is a vital energy for you, because it is the energy of the new era. It is an energy which brings you a strength and a certainty that you are part of the oneness of everything. That is the most important thing you have to achieve, and with this conscious connection outside the world you can become totally transformed. It is the external connection which will become important for you. Until now you have not really been conscious of it. From now on it will be a guiding light for you in all that you do. Look up to the stars, open your awareness, connect with the moon and the sun, look upwards, look outwards, reach up, stretch up, make the connection. Do this in your circles and we will empower you.

43

NEW ELECTRICITY

We are a new element of energy, which has so far been unrecognised, but which in future will be very useful to mankind. We are a special sort of energy which can be applied in daily life to generate ordinary electricity and power. It will not be in the same way that electricity is used now. It is a different form but, nonetheless, useful.

You could say we are a refined form of electricity – we are like petrol compared with crude oil. In future, you will use this rather superior grade of 4-star electricity, with much wider applications than the power used today. In the context you can understand, we have an energy source which is capable of practical day-to-day use, but can also be used in the human aspect for health, and in the spiritual aspect for spiritual health. At the moment, there is great divergence between the crude electricity which you use and the much finer form of electricity which exists in all living matter. The two are more or less incompatible; you cannot stimulate growth with crude mains electricity. You should understand that electricity also exists in a more rarefied form, which can be used for life-enhancing purposes.

It is rather like comparing ordinary sun-light with a laser generated by a ruby crystal. It is the refinement, the organisation, the re-alignment, the coherence, which is the relevant factor. If electricity could be reorganised and disciplined and made much more 'coherent', you would find that it developed a much finer frequency response. The two electrical types that exist now – the 'living' electricity and the crude electricity which you generate – would then come into harmony.

We bring you this message because there is concern in the world about use of fossil fuels. The electricity we are talking about is much more productive, so you will need much smaller quantities of it to achieve the required results for heating, locomotion and even surgical and medical purposes. In future, the amount you need to generate will be greatly reduced. It will come about by the application of research which is already known, but not yet understood. The research is there and the anomalies of electrical behaviour have been noted, but not understood. They have not been seen in context. They have been viewed as an anomaly, or a quirk, but it has not yet been understood that quirks are the keys to major breakthroughs in understanding, in the same way that understanding the quirk of space-time was the key to understanding the major breakthrough of quantum physics.

It would be of no use for us to give it to you, so obviously we are trying to influence those people who are able to understand its application. We come to you, really, as a gesture of goodwill, so that you may not feel too much anxiety about the state of the world.

All energy is one. The sun's energy originates from the same source that all electrical energy originates from. That, too, is part of the key to understanding.

The limitations of nuclear power have already been understood; what has not been understood is the alternative. The alternative will become available within twenty years, say. Like most things it will start in a small, experimental way, and will not be appreciated for the future that it holds. That is normal.

So my friends, we are somehow an embodiment, or expression, or cooperation, and communion with the energy resources which are around and are available; we are something like a voltmeter, we are the registration of that energy.

44

NEW POWER

I am a new force for you – yet another new force. I come to you from the outer world, the experimental world, the world of power, the world of new energy. You are coming to the brink of the new era. I am the power, I am the new force, and you will be able to understand the importance of this. You are already looking for a new source of energy. The world is searching, but it is not ready for the ideas which will be used in the future. I am that new power. I am the source of a great new energy which will be available for mankind when he is ready for it. Unfortunately he is not ready yet.

I come, therefore, to give you some encouragement. The encouragement is that after the change-over, when it seems that the pursuit of fossil fuels will bring the world to its knees, ultimately there will be a resolution. There is a great new source of power which can be used in the future and this will allow mankind to abandon his pursuit. It will allow the world to recover, and allow the whole ecosystem to fall back into equilibrium. It will also mean that mankind will slowly shrink in numbers. The new energy will not allow great numbers of people to use it, but those who do will have a tremendous source of power at their disposal.

I hope you understand that I am trying to say that only those who learn to use the new power will be able to attune to it. Those who cannot learn to use it will inevitably wither away and will not bother to incarnate in the future, so the world population will shrink back to a manageable size and the world will, therefore, be on a path to recovery. So I am telling you not to become fearful about the future. Relax and enjoy the pattern of evolution, change and apparent destruction. All is not what it seems, and I bring you great hope because we are so powerful that everything is within our scope to be managed.

So cast away your despair, and the negative thoughts which are generated by despair, and relax and enjoy the feeling and the understanding of the greater knowledge which I bring to you.

45

NEW THOUGHT ENERGY

We are coming for a second time. We are the new power you met recently. We came to you before in a revelatory vein; this time we come with more understanding and detail for you.

Last time we said that the new power is something that not everyone can attune to. It is a combined power – it will be effective as a replacement for your existing electrical power but also as a direct power for life in terms of stimulating mankind and the other kingdoms. This gives you some idea that these two are not separate energies. They are one and the same thing, but acting on different voltages. They need to be transformed, when you have learned how they can become interchangeable.

When we introduce ourselves as the new power, we are not really new at all, but we are a new perception and new understanding; we are in effect the transformer. So this power brings out the idea of universality – when we say that the life force is everything, we mean just that. This life force is expressed in human terms, in animal, mineral and vegetable terms and also in terms of the motive power with which you are already familiar, to drive your computers, electrical implements and so forth. It is all one and the same thing.

This concept is really quite startling. It will not be understood for another twenty years or so, but ultimately realisation will come. When it does, you will have the possibility of immense interaction between man and machine. Pause for a moment to think of the consequences of that. You have been told before that thought is everything. When you begin to understand that the power of thought and the life force are ultimately one and the same thing, and that those two aspects of mankind can stimulate and control all other motive power, you will begin to understand what we are talking about. This will be the ultimate understanding of the universal force.

Until this time arrives, mankind's understanding of various forces will still be fragmented. Once he has made the mental step towards understanding the interdependence and interchangeability of the two aspects of force, all the other understanding will fall into place. Concepts about the structure of matter will then be revealed as simply an expression of power, which is an expression of the life force, which is an expression of thought. Understanding that matter is a thought will finally arrive.

We have always said that "in the beginning was the thought", although it was perhaps hard to understand the mechanics of what we explained. Once this understanding is achieved, this will be the last link in the chain of understanding between thought and matter. Pause for a moment again and think of the consequences of that also.

The consequences of linking matter with thought will reveal the need for a revolutionary approach to thought. This is closely bound up with the changes mankind (and the rest of the world) will experience during the next twenty years. Unless that revolution of thought takes place, the consequences for both energy and matter could be catastrophic. However, that transformation will happen and those who cannot change will not be around to be involved.

It is also important to understand the necessity for mankind in general (and in particular those with whom you are in contact) to begin transforming his thought patterns. Patterns and vibrational levels of thought must be changed; negativity must be quietly transformed. All of these things must take place. It is not an optional extra; it is crucial. However, once this has happened, the consequences can be startling, brilliant and spectacular. The control of matter will become an everyday occurrence: the science of it will be understood and not regarded as magic. However, the consequences of misusing thought will be horrendous, The social cohesion and the discipline required to maintain high vibrational levels of positive thought will become paramount. Understanding harmony of thought and harmony of mankind will become the central issue of life. You understand, therefore, that love plays a dramatic part in this because love is the mainspring, and the aspect which ultimately controls the patterns of thought. So love is the fundamental aspect we now need to address.

That will be addressed more fully in a while. In the meantime we hope we are building the foundations for this understanding.

46

HARMONY

We are a new Devic spirit for you. We come with a new purpose which is the expression of the golden or harmonic mean. We are the harmony of the spheres; we are the celestial music. However, we also have a much more specific role. We represent the beautiful harmony which exists in a continuous form for those who can hear it. This harmony is an expression of the ultimate; it is the totality and the unification of that ultimate expression. That harmony is a symbol of the expression of unity. Disharmony is disunity. Thus harmony in music, in tune, tone and in sound are vitally important.

We have a role to play which consists of bringing together a new harmonic expression to match the new age. Traditional harmonies have been recognised by man and animals as 'true' and were right for their times, but with the changing of the era, new harmonies will be evolved which will be recognised as being true for the new times. They will be different from the past. There is no simple immutable harmony that applies for ever.

At the moment you are losing the recognition of the old harmony but, so far, you fail to understand the new harmony. The consequence, therefore, is cacophony. The cacophony is healthy because it recognises that the old harmonies, however beautiful, were only an expression of their own times. The new harmonies will become expressions of the new times. The cacophony is the breaking down of the old order and is essential for the evolution of the new order. You cannot have a new tune while the old tune is still playing.

So now we are going through an interesting stage. You will become sufficiently evolved that you can hear and recognise the harmonies of the new age. Initially you will hear them non-physically – not in your waking state but in your trance or sleep state and in higher consciousness. Although you will not hear them in your waking state, you will ultimately begin to recognise those harmonic echoes in the physical world, that is, physical sounds will remind you of the harmonies of the new age.

They will become important, and not merely trivial or background music. They will be your life and soul, like the very life force that floods through you. It will be impossible to imagine life without the new harmony. The new harmony and the new life will be completely intertwined. They will not be separate packages for separate occasions, but more part and parcel of the expression of the new life. It will be important to recognise how important this is. It will not be something to listen to occasionally but will become so integral that you will not be able to function without simultaneously tuning to this harmony as an expression of love. It will be as the way you love. You will not, for example, be able to walk down the street without love – you need to walk with love and with harmony. You will not be able to separate yourselves from it.

47

COSMIC ENERGY

We came to you before, when you were not quite ready to pursue our ideas, but now the era has changed and we can come to you again with an expanded concept. We are talking about a new energy of quite a different sort; we are talking about the energy of the spheres. The energy we talked about before was a cosmic energy. We mentioned it briefly, but we did not linger on it. The cosmic energy that we represent is a new force which you have not experienced before. It is outside your daily experience.

The cosmic energy comes through to you from outside the Earth. Everything else you experience comes from within the Earth; even the effects of the moon and the sun are sensed from the energy reflected from the Earth. The cosmic energy we are talking about comes directly from outside, and it comes to you with a direct purpose.

You can sense this energy in a variety of ways – you sense it in the life force which you feel, you sense it in your mental stimulation, you sense it in your etheric stimulation – but all of these things are secondary. The primary stimulation you receive is through your psyche, as it were, through your soul.

So I think you see a connection with what we have said before. When you wish to energise yourselves, or to create a greater force, you need to draw upon the cosmic energy over and above your own human energy, or the plant, mineral and vegetable energies around you; you need to draw on us. We can provide you with an energy source which transcends everything you have experienced up until now, The energy source we can provide would be equivalent to 100,000 volts compared with the little 12-volt battery which you are now operating. The energy is the great source of all power outside your solar system; it is beyond the solar system. We are not talking about your own solar system or even the beings behind the sun; we are the source from outside and we exist outside your own universe.

We are a universal energy source which permeates the cosmos, but because the source is not from within your own system, you will understand that this power is all encompassing; this is the universal force, the universal energy which permeates the entire cosmos – nothing parochial. The energy that we offer is special because of its universality. Being universal, this energy is the very finest and purest vibrational level you can experience.

The energy source is all around you, and it permeates you; but because of the fineness of its vibrational level, it has not been very easy to draw upon. You must now start to train your own psyches to become aware of this energy, to breathe it in, draw upon it, recycle it and to charge your world with it. You are bidden to take advantage of this universal cosmic energy, to stimulate and charge the world around you – both your fellow man and all the surrounding life force. It is a unique opportunity.

This is not an experience which has happened generally or in any widespread form before, but the opportunity now exists, for the first time ever, to absorb this new energy, because your vibrational level will be changing to a pitch at which can finally accommodate it. This is an opportunity for which mankind has been waiting for many millennia. The moment is about to arise. You need to practise; you need to be ready for it. You need to be, as it were, trained to handle the stimulating power of this new cosmic force.

Inevitably, the first step is to become aware. The first step is to ask the question, "what does it feel like?" You will be given the answer: you will be given the sensation. You will get to know the sensation, you will feel it, you will breathe it in. Like the Prana, it is sensitive to the in-breath, not because it is in the air but because, by breathing it in, you stimulate those vital centres within you which are most susceptible to the energy. To summarise therefore, first ask to feel it; practise breathing in; practise the sensation that you receive when you breathe in. Become aware of the force, become aware of the effect of your inward breath. Breathe in the force, breathe in the power.

Secondly, once you have breathed it in, become aware of it, feel it, sense it; become, as it were, attuned to it. Become stimulated by it, become aware of the stimulating sensation which it creates. You will be aware that it is different from the universal life force – this is not the same thing. The cosmic energy which we bring will transform the physical life energy provided by the life force whom you have met before. So the cosmic energy is over and above, it is the supercharging energy of the life force. It will transform the life force from the mundane to the transcendental.

The third way you will begin to use us is that, having become aware of the sensation of the power which it generates within you, and having become aware of your enhanced life force, you will then be able to feel the effects flowing outwards from you. You will become the transformers that we talked about before. You will become transformers of cosmic energy. You will be able to transmit energy and power to those around you on a slightly reduced level.

You will have taken the cosmic energy, transformed it, utilised it, and given out an energy to your fellow man. This is the energy you will need for the next era. This is the energy which you need to transform your vibrational level. It will be the stimulus to change gear. It will be the cosmic energy which beams in to make the changes possible.

48

THE WORLD ENERGY FORCE

Greetings! We are a new energy force for you. We come to you with a particularly important message. The world energy field that I represent is the logic for the next stage of evolution. We are the logic, the reason, the matrix. When you build your energy network of human Light, we are able to attach ourselves to those centres and draw energy from them. It is an energy which we can transform to a higher level of vibration. So when you are active, you must be aware that you produce consequent energies in a form which we can utilise.

The word 'Gaia' has been used. This is not directly our energy, but we are the matrix, or the logic which controls the Gaia. We are the fundamental world energy which controls evolution, and holds the world balance and pattern. For this reason, the network you build both forms the safety net for mankind, and is simultaneously the powerhouse which generates and controls the energy field.

We hope, therefore, that you will understand the significance of this. We control the energies which are fed through into the mineral kingdom. The mineral kingdom itself feeds the animal kingdom and the vegetable kingdom, but it is the human kingdom which feeds us. Therefore you represent a link in the cyclical exchange of energies.

You must understand that as the transformation happens, we ourselves will be changing too. We will change our structure, and we will cease to be an overgrid. Instead, in the future, we will somehow interpenetrate the world. We will then be much more accessible and immediate for you. Similarly, we will need your energy to a much greater extent than hitherto. We hope that you will be able to work with us in the next few decades to effect this transformation.

The power which we can give you will help. It will bring about the transformation of consciousness, it will make the transition easier, and it will increase understanding. But it is crucial that, together with this consciousness, you develop an understanding of the importance of your input for us. Therefore, when we say that the grid you create is important, you now begin to get a glimpse of the vital nature of the evolutionary pattern which it generates.

We would like to be with you on several occasions in the future, and to communicate with you. We hope that you will be feeding us directly as much as you can. I would suggest that while feeding the network, you bring the world energy field into mind; allow this energy, as it were, to bridge the gap between us. I ask you to do this in all humility. I hope that you will be able to spread the word as much as possible and indicate the importance of this union. You will recognise us through our symbol, which is the helical spiral. That is really all I have to say.

49

THE SPIRIT OF THE NEW AGE

We have come to you before – the spirit of the new age. We have given you a few shimmering glimpses of what it is about, but it was not possible to begin until we were complete and the impetus needed to gather before we could really talk about it. However, the time has come – you are complete and the film is rolling.

The first stage is going to be one of considerable change. The new age is happening now. The physical world is changing already. The economic changes which flow from this will begin in about a year. You can expect considerable economic change – not necessarily hardship, I must repeat that, do not have an attitude of doom and gloom to this; just as a marketplace can be quiet or bullish, in the same way the economic environment will become incredibly active. That is not necessarily all bad or all good – just a tremendous amount of change.

So you can expect to see rapid change, formation, dissolution and so on – markets suddenly collapsing and rebuilding, industries disappearing and new ones starting up. We are talking about an economic change which is a consequence of the fabric change, if you like. On a very crude level, you will find gluts in some products and scarcity in others and that will have a dramatic effect on the market forces of the world. It is inevitable that you will go through this period of very rapid economic change.

But that is only scratching the surface of the problem because, following about a year after that, in two to three years' time, you will begin (as always) to see cultural, political and philosophical ideas following the reality of the marketplace. It is not necessarily that the market follows the ideas; very often the market serves as a rapid indicator of changes taking place, and only after the event do people actually sit down to analyse what has happened. The culture of one age was the novelty art of the previous age, and that is a recognition of a change that has already taken place. Similarly, in two or three years' time you will see the cultural recognition of the changes that are taking place now.

Initially there will be confusion and lack of understanding, but shortly after that will come ideas; people will start to draw the strings together to make sense of what is taking place. They will try to establish the themes and understand the pattern of events. But they will get it wrong. Inevitably they will start to ascribe complex reasons for the change and, as usual, they will miss the point – the point being that there is far more involved than they realise. People will always use the pattern of previous experience to explain the present and predict the future. Inevitably people's previous experiences, almost by definition, will be wide of the mark. Maybe a generation later people will see that their ideas were quite inappropriate and they were trying to tackle major changes with inadequate tools of perception and understanding.

That is the cultural and philosophical change which will follow. But during all this time you will have changes of vibrational level taking place despite the economic and political turmoil, and despite the philosophical and cultural manoeuvring that will follow. In a sense the intuitive understanding of large numbers of people will have already accommodated the changes, so the theorising and cultural ideas which will follow will be a crystallisation of the intuitive understanding which has already come from a vibrational level. This huge leap in understanding will happen on an intuitive or subconscious level.

Perversely, you will find true intuitive understanding even when the cultural explanations of conventional wisdom will not have grasped what is happening. For example, you are beginning to see a new awareness of the true importance of the Earth and the environment around us — that in itself is not wholly explicable in logical terms. It is a product of a changing awareness and not necessarily of increasing damage to the environment; it is more a product of heightened awareness about that environment.

So my friends, that is really what I wanted to say. We will keep regular contact with you so that you can, as it were, compare notes during the period of incremental change.

We are the spirit of the new age, and we will be watching you.

50

THE TRANSFORMING LIGHT

We come with a new aspect again. The way we will work with you is through the ultimate experience. You know that you have the power in you to change the world. You know it in a sense, and yet you do not accept it. You have the power to influence other people in a way that you do not give yourself credit for. You are not prepared to take the risk. We come to you with an energy which has not really been voiced or expressed before. I am only the messenger for that energy, I am not the energy itself. The energy that I symbolise is the energy with which you can transform other people.

You know that time is running out for your old existence in which you were afraid, embarrassed or somehow constrained to come out and speak the truth. In the past you have felt that you were not important enough to be able to make a significant difference. I hope that, with our help, you may realise what power you have at your fingertips. Wherever you see a situation or a collection of ideas which you know are retrograde, and which could be transformed with Light, or where you recognise a soul searching for the truth, then know that you have the power to transform them.

I say to you, go out and do it; do not sit and back any more, please, I beg you – that time has gone. When you meet this situation, all you need to do is to summon up the power that I have for you and simply remember me as a symbol, as a messenger for this power, Call on me: I will transmit it for you, I will bring you any amount of power that you need. All you need to do is to direct it, transform it, beam it out, and then those areas, those people, those souls, those minds, those attitudes, will be transformed. We can do it together. Without you we are powerless. Without us you are powerless.

We are the Light, but that does not say it all. We are the Light very specifically required and charged with the duty of transformation. The transforming Light. All we ask of you is to call on us.

51

THE SPIRIT OF THE ENVIRONMENT

We are now going to tell you something quite new. We are going to tell you about the changes to the environment. There has been much talk recently about the perils and the dangers to the environment, and I am going to tell you that the environment is going to be radically altered. When I talk to you about the environment I mean basically the air that you breathe, the water you drink, the ground that you walk on, and all the natural kingdoms.

You have become part of a society which adopts the view that man has a responsibility for the environment. That is a new idea. The environment on the other hand has not yet taken up the idee that man has this responsibility. The environment believes, as it always has, that it is a self-regulating system and is able to cope quite nicely, thank you. It has not yet accepted the idea that man is somehow responsible for it, and therefore in charge of it.

The change now about to take place is in the fact that the environment itself (I mean of course all the Devic energies that are involved in the environment) is going to go through a metamorphosis; they are all part of the evolution and are going to make a similar change to mankind. You could say that mankind has led the way with his change of awareness.

However, mankind's change of awareness towards the environment is only a first step. The change in the future will be that man, instead of viewing himself as responsible for the environment, will change his approach to the idea that man and his environment are one; they are indivisible, they are not separate. It is not as though man is the parent and the environment is the child; they will be as one person.

The environment will then have a completely different response. The Devas, instead of sensing some sort of patronage, will perceive an equal partnership. They will perceive a union in which they can participate. Once that takes place, the environment will change beyond recognition because it will become interactive. It will become responsive to man's input and his intentions. For example, if man shows a positive intention to take care of a particular aspect then the environment will, in the future, positively respond to this care and attention. It will be like two lovers.

This time is not far away; we are talking about five to ten years. It is a very short space of time for all the natural kingdoms to make this change, and it will be a quantum leap for them, perhaps even greater than for mankind. The fact that the natural kingdom will be able and willing, and positively encouraging this responsiveness and environmental two-way dialogue, will be one of the most exciting things of the next step in the evolutionary cycle.

I bring you this as a measure of hope and excitement through this rather gloomy intermediate stage of man's perception, My friends, I hope this is of interest and rings a bell in your mind. Thank you, I will bid you farewell. As a representative of all the nature kingdoms, I am a spokesman.

52

THE SPIRIT OF CHANGE

We are pleased to be able to talk to you. We have something special to say, which is basically that we are a power for introducing change. We have expressed ourselves in the past in a slightly different format, but we are the entity of change. We have a role which is brought into action at the end of each cycle, when the new era is about to be entered. We become activated and instigate those areas of change which will stimulate the transition from one era from another.

I want to say to you that the role that we have adopted for the change of this particular cycle is a new one for us. In the past the changes which occurred on the passing of the cycles (approximately every two thousand years) have been like those of an 'agent provocateur' – we have become involved in the world and we have, as it were, pressed the triggers in society; we have become the catalysts of society. We have joined with those individuals who have been the champions of change,

On this occasion, however, things are different – we have a slightly modified role to play and I need to explain how it will work. On this occasion we will work by merging with all of you who can absorb our rather uncomfortable vibrations. That is to say, as an energy, we will be completely diffused, not at all focused. We will be like some liquid which will spread over the world and can be absorbed by particularly porous people. It will be the pieces of blotting paper who will soak up the liquid, while individuals with hard glossy surfaces will be less susceptible to this penetration. That will be the way we choose to work on this occasion. It will be very different from before.

That means, therefore, that individuals like yourselves will be able to absorb our energy. We can tell you that, in this respect, all of you are simply very porous pieces of blotting paper! It means that you will be able to absorb the energy which we bring and you will be able to feel the change when others cannot.

I am telling you this because you have a very distinct role to play. You can focus this energy by becoming aware of us and by clearly formulating in your own mind a consciousness of the energy soaking into you, as it interpenetrates you and becomes a part of your very being. You can understand that once you are made aware of this energy you can operate in a very different way. You can sense, you can feel, you can become invigorated by this energy for change. Once you become aware of it you will never be afraid of it.

On the other hand, if you were to try to operate without awareness, you could easily become quite disorientated and very fearful. That would be completely destructive for yourselves and for the heralding of the new era. So I simply come to your awareness; I bring myself into your conscious recognition and ask that you hold the awareness of the subtle energy in your mind. Become aware of us, acknowledge us and become infused by us and enthused by us.

That is all I really needed to say. I look forward to being soaked up.

53

ENERGY OF THE NEW AGE

We are the energy of the New Age. Our specific task is to introduce the ideas of the New Age to those who can understand them.

The New Age has its own controlling entities. We are an expression of that entity. We are not a human energy. We have our own power, we have our own structure, and we have our own organisational aspects, but what I wish to say is that the energy itself needs to be understood; it is not sufficient to accept the idea that there is an energy and that everything will be all right, because this will not allow you to absorb the power, which we can offer quickly enough.

The aspect of the New Age I am talking about is the speed of change (in your terms). It is important that as many people as possible can understand and accommodate this energy so that they can be influenced by it rather than simply washed over by it. The sooner you actually adjust to the different vibrational frequency the sooner you can become of use to other people – the sooner you can become distributors of that energy, and transmitters of that power to those around you.

I say this advisedly, but we would be extremely grateful if each of you would allow a conscious period of time to acclimatise to this new vibrational frequency. If you spend five minutes a day it would achieve everything – that is all that is required, but the essence of the five minutes is to be wholly devoted to attuning to the new frequency. If you do that and if, in that short time, you bring the conscious intent to link with us, we could all make the transition within weeks. Think of the consequences of that.

My friends, we would be delighted to work with you and we hope that you would consider the challenge. We will be there and we hope you will be too.

54

ENERGY OF THE PISCEAN AGE

We are the old energy from the previous age. We come to bid you farewell. We wish to cast a fleeting backward glance at the previous age, just as you yourselves would, on dying, cast a backward glance over the purpose and the achievement of your previous life.

We of course are the Piscean Age. What we wished to achieve, when we started out, was the development of the human condition, particularly his condition. This has been the age of mankind. It was to develop a particular aspect of mankind, namely the dimension of compassion. The fundamental goal of the whole age was that ability, which man alone possesses, to take upon himself the joy and suffering of another. That is a specifically human attribute.

As far as achievement is concerned, we would suggest that is has only been about sixty percent successful. In the closing years of the era there has been a huge growth of awareness of the rights, sensibilities and feelings of others. The whole concept of communism, socialism and similar philosophies is based on the idea that other people's feelings and sensibilities are just as important as our own. That was quite a novel idea (in terms of thousands of years). It was a very new idea not to concentrate solely on one's own sensations, thoughts and feelings.

This has been accompanied by another dramatic change which goes in parallel, which is, of course, the evolution of individual responsibility – that perhaps is the area in which we have had most success. The whole concept of democracy assumes that individuals must take responsibility. It is not acceptable simply to do as one is told. That is again a dramatic new departure. It can only be conceived within the current age – it could not have been contemplated in previous eras.

Thirdly, we have the whole aspect of interdependence. As a result of highly complex political, social and economic structures, interdependence now means that if you destroy another man, you yourself become diminished. That is also a novel aspect.

In those three areas, therefore, we have had some modicum of success. The areas that have been failures, if you like, are the reverse side (the negative side) of each of these three aspects. I would say that the problem, in terms of the compassion, has been that in pursuing one's concept of what is right, many people have become so fixated that they have been unable to see other points of view. This has resulted in awful dogma, political and national pride, resulting in catastrophic warfare.

To take the third aspect next, the whole concept of interdependence has its own negative side, in a sense, because interdependence has been bred only with the cost of developing competitiveness. This was not part of the plan. We wanted interdependence without intense competition for ideas, for money, for resources, or for living space, for status, and for everything you can imagine, The idea of competition is not necessary, and was not originally envisaged.

And then the last aspect – the negative side of coming together as individuals with responsibility has meant that with the relaxing of control, individuals have the free will to create chaos for the rest of mankind! Inevitably there has been a percentage of individuals who have taken the liberty without the corresponding responsibility; that, I suppose you could say, was inevitable.

And so we bid farewell to the previous era with mixed feelings, of partial achievements and many failures. The many failures will continue in the new era until they are resolved, so unfortunately you will be going into the new era with some unfinished business, some residue still to be sublimated. It will not make the next stage any easier, of course.

55

ENERGY COORDINATING THE KINGDOMS

We are a new energy again – yet another energy. My function is the resolution of disharmony and the dissolution of the tension caused by unresolved energies.

We operate, generally, within the Earth's level but our influence extends both up and down. Under the circumstances therefore we resolve the energies of all the kingdoms. You will find that energy conflicts build up between individuals of the same kingdom, between groups of individuals in the same kingdoms, and finally between nations and continents. Similarly, localised tensions and disharmonies will build up between different kingdoms, for example between the human and the mineral kingdom or between the human and animal kingdom. These disharmonies arise because of a lack of understanding and because one element chooses to hold itself apart. That state of affairs is not only unnatural but also extremely unhelpful. Separation is an illness. Separation from one's environment is an illness of the soul.

We cannot impose a resolution and we cannot impose a harmonisation – the only way we can work is by creating a realisation. There are two ways we do this. The first way is to create an environment where the overriding importance of harmony becomes self-evident – not only self-evident but also very desirable and very attractive. We try to make it an attractive idea as far as those elements are concerned. I am not only talking about the human kingdom: this applies equally to the Devic kingdom, the mineral kingdom, the plant kingdom, the gnomes and the elves and all the other controlling energies which can sometimes develop this fear – and fear is a separation.

The other way we operate is to bring about circumstances which are so traumatic that the need for harmonisation and union (the loss of separateness) just becomes self-evident. To get to that stage of course means that things have to become fairly bad before the individual kingdoms are forced to change. That is if you like the 'stick' approach as oppose to the former 'carrot' approach.

You will understand that we are now becoming particularly involved in the next stage of evolution. We are one of the prime energies working, unseen and out of view, but really controlling the pace of events. We are trying to create this house of cards; we are juggling with all the energies simultaneously. We hope that we can achieve our purposes by the 'carrot' method. To do so we need all the help we can get.

We ask of you in great humility whether you are able to help us. We need the union, and the concept of union, which you can offer when you reach out to the other kingdoms. That will diffuse many of the tensions which have already arisen between, for example, man and the animal kingdom, or between man and the vegetable kingdom. Those tensions are in desperate need of resolution.

As you work with your networks, and as you form the union with the other kingdoms, we are able to utilise the energy you generate and transmute it for the other kingdoms. You are not simply working on your own, because we immediately plug into any energy that you generate. My friends, we ask you to do all you can to generate that energy; as you do so, hold in mind the end which we wish to achieve. If you do so we will be empowered to create the transition peacefully and without threat.

56

THE ANGELIC CONTROL

Well, we are now ready to start on a new phase with you. We are the energy of the angel – very appropriate considering you 'are asking the question. When I identify ourselves like this I am really saying that we do not have a specific role in the Devic kingdom in the way they have been introduced so far. We operate on a diffused level – we are the controllers, we are the instigators, we are the trigger mechanism. We control the rate of change. In the past we have introduced you to other aspects of ourselves. We have introduced you to the regulators who in turn respond to us. Those aspects have already talked about how they work.

We, on the other hand, are the source of the control. We are the ultimate operating controller. It is our energy force which is now allowing the change to take place in a modulated and well-regulated manner. It is time, therefore, to advise you that you have now completed the first phase of the change. The first phase (which you have been living through for the last 10 months) has been in full flood but was still basically a preparatory stage. You know that many things have happened in the last 10 months. The world is a totally different place from the one you were living in this time last year; that is evident. What you now need to take on board is the idea that this was only setting the scene.

The really exciting part is about to begin. It will start in two months time. You will see some changes in the world taking place on several levels. The political changes will be rather cataclysmic – that is to say it will not be all sweetness and light. The political changes, however, will only be taking place on the surface of things. The economic changes will be equally dramatic. You should be aware that the present state of affairs cannot continue – you know that, and it is a matter of timing. But more importantly the change in people's minds has only just begun and that will be the most important aspect to change during the next 10 to 12 months.

We think that you have an opportunity to disseminate a greater understanding of what is going on to the people you come in contact with. We rely on you to use this information and to spread it to those who can use it. You must give people the idea that this change is not a disaster, it is not an accident and it is only the beginning. Only if you take on board the idea that the cataclysmic aspect of the evolution is desirable rather than frightening can you actually derive any positive benefit from it at all.

We now have the opportunity to meet you on more than one occasion. We would like to return to you regularly throughout the next 12 months to bring to you an understanding of each stage of the evolution. You will be able to ask us questions on each occasion to fill out your understanding of what is happening in your own part of the world – in your own little sphere. We would welcome the interchange which you could bring on future occasions. We hope that this will be part of a new phase of communication between yourselves and the controlling entities.

It is an opportunity which has not really been available to you or others before. It is only because the state of change has come to such a pitch and because your own evolution has progressed sufficiently that you are able to make this contact at all.

I think, my friend, that that is all we need to say on this first introductory session. We hope to meet you again, and that will be the opportunity for a greater exchange of ideas. Thank you for your patience, and I bid you good night.

57

ENERGY OF THE CHANGES

The energy I bring to you is that of the power of regeneration. We are the energy which pervades the Earth and brings about the changes in such a way that it allows for new growth rather than simply refurbishment. We are the energy which will suffuse the planet in about twenty years' time, when the state of the environment has become so acute that an acknowledgement of us will be needed to bring us into the scene – so we have an immensely powerful role.

We take on the role of the rejuvenator and we create the rebirth and growth of those aspects of life that have become tarnished by the spiritual and environmental decline brought about by ignorance, so you could call us the ultimate spirit of the environment, but of course, this includes a much wider interpretation than is normally given to that word.

Our role, therefore, is to rescue the world – no mean undertaking – but the reason that we are here tonight, rather prematurely, is because you are one of the few groups able to understand what is to take place. You, therefore, have a great responsibility to bring about an awareness of what can be achieved in spite of the destruction apparent all around. There will be great fear, there will be great pessimism and great doom and gloom, but because you know of our existence you will have the power to reinforce the positive aspect – which is, that regrowth is possible and regrowth will take place because you have come to know us.

We ask you, therefore, to start work now in laying the foundations for this understanding. You have the power to do it, you have the wherewithal to do it; you can spread the knowledge through the network, you can use the crystal energy to intensify the dissipation of this knowledge. You have everything you need at your disposal, and we ask you please to prepare the way for us.

58

THE SPIRIT OF THE FUTURE

I come to you with great power, certainly, but also a great feeling of weight. The reason for this is that we come from the future – a difficult concept for you to understand. We therefore feel a great weight being in the present. The frequency you operate on feels to us like wearing lead boots.

I give you the idea of lightness; that as you go forward through the next 25 years (those of you who are going to stick around), the feeling will become quite spectacular. The frequency that we operate on is like the highest note you can hear compared with the deepest organ note. That is the range that we will be presenting to you.

So I have to say to you, my friends, that you need to learn to lighten your feeling. You need to learn the lighter frequencies. As you meditate, I would recommend that you go through a series of sequential exercises which, as it were, take the present vibration and gradually wind it up to a new frequency step by step so that you both lift yourself up and lift the environment up with you. Like that you will learn the feel of the new frequency before you are smitten by it.

That will be a tremendous help for you, but, more importantly, it will be a tremendous help for those with whom you come into contact. I strongly recommend that you carry out this sequential series of exercises and we will be there in order to give you the familiar feeling as you begin to recognise what we are talking about.

My friends, I hope that the next few times you meet you will deliberately and consciously carry out this exercise.

59

PRANA

We are now going to give you a small taste or appetiser of the way you will be in three years' time. We are the new Prana, the Prana which has existed since time immemorial. The Prana itself is the life force that you breathe and which generates life; it creates the difference between life and death. We are that Prana, but in common with the rest of the world's evolution, we will be subtly changing our vibration frequency. It has already started in a small way, but during the next twelve months our operating frequency will be radically altered.

Within the next two years the significance of that change will become tangible and sensible to you. You will find that the breathing pattern you adopt will have a dramatic and significant effect on the way you feel and tune to the other life energies on the planet. We would suggest that you take the opportunity to carry out some very specific and careful breathing exercises – probably once a month, maybe in the group but certainly as individuals. I can give you a clue:

The breathing exercises I would suggest are firstly that you form a very clear, almost visual, mental image of the Prana life force. In your mind's eye, perceive the Prana life force as the crucial element in your physical being and visualise slowly breathing in that life force with very slow, absorbing breaths, lasting for 10 to 15 seconds. During that exercise you can perceive the Light energy penetrating your body and being absorbed by every single pore, vein and vessel in your body. Perceive the Light energy being absorbed totally and, after a minute or two, as you progress with the exercise, you will gradually feel this energy changing subtly. It will not be the energy changing, it will be your perception of the energy that changes; your perception will recognise that the energy is, in fact, a finer, higher subtle frequency.

So, as you continue your breathing exercises and as you breathe in, visualise not only the Prana being absorbed, but also this heightened awareness happening at the same time. As you do so you will feel a remarkable change taking place throughout your system. It will have a physical effect, but it will also have a mental and an emotional effect which will happen every single moment. The absorption of this new Prana will become disproportionately significant in the next two or three years. I ask you therefore to do this exercise once a month in the group in order to reinforce the idea of your own mental consciousness in your approach to the evolutionary transition. I ask you to be quite methodical and systematic about this, because it is easy to forget.

In a year's time you will find that the Prana is subtly altered, and the effect on you will be so dramatic that you will feel that you are floating two or three inches off the ground when you do this exercise. You may find it a little disorientating, but do not be concerned – it is natural and good. It may, for example, make you feel dizzy or disconnected from reality. It will be the normal readjustment of your physical body to the new Prana frequency which you will be absorbing. After a few months you will find that the sense of heightened awareness will feel very normal; it will not feel strange or alien, so please persist.

Once you have gone through this transition, you will find that each of your senses has been heightened to a degree you had not expected. You will find that, for example, your vision will be intensified – you will see things that only Sue can see now. You will hear things you may not have been aware of and you will certainly smell things which only Jane might have smelt up until now. You will have heightened awareness of every single sense.

That heightened awareness is extremely important – treasure it, cherish it, but also be gentle with your self. Do not expose yourself, for example, to extreme noise. Do not expose yourself to ugly sights and smells if you can help it. Your heightened awareness will need a gradual evolution to face up to this higher degree of sensitivity.

This will be a direct result of the change in the Prana frequency. As you carry out your exercises we will be with you, and we hope you will be with us.

60

PRANA CONTROL

We are part of the Prana. We are that magic life ingredient, the Prana entity, the Prana essence. We spoke to you before about the vital nature of our life-giving force. However, we are a rather specialised part of the Prana energy. We provide a subtlety of purpose.

The Prana is the life-giving force – when you breathe the Prana, you are enlivened. In addition, you actually create life; as you take your first breath you start to live as an independent being. Provided you continue to breathe, you will still be alive. When you take your last breath, the life force departs. The life force in this instance is a totally separate energy from your spiritual energies. Spiritual energies can only inhabit a body which is suffused with the life force provided by the Prana.

The Prana itself comes from the atmosphere; it is a subtle component of the atmosphere. We, on the other hand, create a subtlety of purpose within each individual life energy, whether it be human, animal, vegetable or mineral, which is quite distinct, and identifiable for each individual. So, the life energy of every single person has a subtle difference from his neighbour's. Although Prana is a generalised life force, breathed in by everyone, we somehow take that Prana and give it an individual stamp, so the vibrational frequency of each individual is subtly different, and identified by a supply of Prana which we can control.

Therefore, as each individual evolves, he subtly enhances his life energy as a result of his approach to the experiences of life. As he harmonises with the higher energies, we are able to tune the Prana energy ever higher, so that the energy level is adjusted according – to your ability to absorb it. It is not that you actually generate the life energy directly. You absorb the highest frequency you are open to. We supply energy of a frequency that matches your availability or your openness.

So, we have a remarkably integrated relationship with mankind in particular, and with the other forces in general, During the changeover, our role together is going to become increasingly important, because we need to work much more closely than was necessary before. For example, in the past, during the lifetime of an individual, only minor variations or adjustments to your energy frequency were required, Now on the other hand, we hope and trust that you will be making constant and continuous incremental changes, almost every week. This requires your acknowledgement of us, and also a finer tuning by us to your requirements. If you can bring an adjustment and an acknowledgement of our power into your awareness, it will become easier for you to make the adjustments and absorb our subtly changing energy.

There is a need. We hope and we request that during your meditations (which are increasingly important) you will cast a thought or an energy in our direction, because by doing so, you will enhance the connection. You will then enable yourselves to make the change more easily. We hope that we will be in close relationship with you over the coming years, and we hope that our frequencies can be in such a natural relationship that there need never be a problem of imbalance.

My friends, this is very much something which you have within your power to enhance, and we, for our part, will do everything to boost that connectedness.

We are Prana Control. In the last nine months the Prana energy has changed dramatically. The Prana energy is one of the prime instigators of the change. Many of the other energies will follow in consequence, but the Prana energy is one of the few instigators.

Thank you, my friends. I will take my leave.

61

THE LIFE FORCE OF MANKIND

We are now going to give you another new experience. We are the life force. We come to give you a feeling of the true nature of man's essence – not his expression, but his essence.

When you incarnate into this kingdom you are making a conscious decision to evolve. The reason you are making that decision, as you have been told, is to evolve the life force. The life force is in a state of permanent flux. We are able to give mankind a particular direction and that is our main purpose, to provide that evolutionary goal.

So we provide mankind with a very subtle influence. As well as his own soul, mankind has his own group soul with its own individuality and its essential being. The common life force which we represent does not just breathe life into mankind, like some daily energy quotient. We are much more like the pilot light which kindles all the other energies. We are like the source of a true flame. We are the source of the ultimate energy and so we are the fundamental life force of mankind. Our interaction, of course, goes back a long way.

The question which you did not ask, but you will ask eventually, was "When was mankind originally evolved as a separate expression from the more deterministic animal, vegetable and mineral kingdoms?" Now we, the life force, are in fact responsible for that very first breath. The understanding of the biblical expression "Let there be life" – the life referred to here was when we, the life force, actually breathed life into mankind and created a new individuality. So we were the life force which was responsible for the original separation. The original separation was mankind – this is the Garden of Eden symbol. So the Garden of Eden was all nosey until mankind came along – we, the life force, were the responsible agent.

The consequences of all this is that the life force is in fact controlling the destiny of mankind, but this is a generalised destiny. We are not at all interested in the individual destiny of specific nations or individuals at any particular phase of evolution, but the ultimate destiny of mankind is something which we are absolutely involved with. We have a compulsion with it and we would say, to your surprise perhaps, that we are firmly in control of the destiny of mankind. You may ask how this can be when there is free will, but the very fact that we were able to breathe free will into existence in the first place gives you an indication that we can breathe it out again. However we are not inclined to do so because that would be a negation of the ultimate progression which we are seeking. So, we do not choose to deny you free will, but we are inclined to keep a fairly firm control on the direction that free will may take. We will therefore apply all the influences we can summon up to direct man's 'free' choices in certain directions!

So we would say to you, do not despair, because that creates a negative environment. Despairing about the direction of mankind's evolution is the wrong reaction; you should try to cultivate a more positive approach, because that will help us, whereas the negative reaction does not help us at all. Despair about mankind's direction is not a good thing. We need your positive affirmation that the good and positive aspects of mankind can and will be built and evolved. With positive affirmation from you, we can use the energy for that purpose.

We, the life force, are very much involved in providing energies to direct the collective decisions of mankind. Think of mankind again as being like an individual; we are, if you like, that individual's guide. We do not take away the free choice but on occasion we heavily influence him to make things evolve in certain directions.

Being the life force we are, of course, totally committed and involved with the entire energy structure of the world. We do not really see a differentiation between mankind and the world. We see any difference here as a regrettable interlude which will be overcome. Mankind will learn to reunite with the energy and the life force of the world as a whole, if for none other than rather selfish reasons.

Well, my friends, nice to get to know you. We will be around on several occasions and we will always be with you of course.

62

THE EVOLUTION OF MANKIND

We are a new energy source for the evolution of mankind. We are like a giant pendulum or the escapement in a clock; we are the regulator, and the modulator that allows evolution to proceed at a certain rhythm. Our particular responsibility is for the evolution of mankind. This is a problem of course, because mankind has free will and yet we are trying to control his evolution, so we have some minor local difficulties. We are not really in a position to dictate the pace of evolution, but we have a responsibility for setting up the scenario for it.

So we are trying to create an environment in which mankind can make choices to develop at the right pace. Of course a lot of other influences are brought to bear in parallel. We set the scene and we can create particular scenarios for mankind at certain times which will allow him to take advantage of the evolution, which he ought to be sensing from other sources as well.

Not surprisingly, this is just such a moment. We have been setting the scene for the last few years; this consists of preparing the ground by influencing a few specific individuals in certain ways. This is naturally a product of free will. We cannot influence any individual without his specific agreement, but once given that agreement, we can influence people in a rather dramatic way. We call ourselves the instigators; we are the precipitators, the catalysts, and we do this by influencing individuals who can dare to pronounce certain novel ideas, and whose role is to open up the general awareness of mankind.

The people who are directly influenced can voice the unthinkable; they can speak ideas which have not been thought before. Of course they receive nothing but ridicule, as ever, but this does not matter because the ridicule itself lends power to that thought, which simply ignoring it would not. In a perverse and ironic way the ridicule these individuals receive generates the instigation of change.

So this is how we work, and we have been very busy recently. Many people have received a lot of ridicule, but that phase is almost over; what happens next will be a quantum flip from one direction to the next, when the body of opinion will move surprisingly fast to the ideas that had previously been held only by those who were thought to be crazy eccentrics.

And you have been receiving this influence whether you realise it or not. You were predisposed to the influence and you each recognised the source.

There is more ridicule to come, but you will not mind because you know that within a relatively short time, instead of being a minority view you will become the majority view. You will rightly feel that you have in a small way been responsible for that change.

The situation is that people's attitudes have actually changed faster than the established wisdom. This is a reversal of the traditional role when the educated were supposedly more progressive than, for example, the peasants. The situation is now reversed, so that the degree of change and the level of understanding has progressed further in the general population than with their so-called elders and betters in positions of public authority. Now there is a reversal of the traditional situation.

This is why the change, when it comes, will appear to be so sudden. The changes are going on rather consistently, but they will appear to be sudden because the public profile will appear to shift quickly, catching up with the change which has been going on at a day-to-day level with ordinary folk. We suspect that if you were able to take a poll of the views of the ordinary men and women in this country about their true beliefs in terms of spiritual development, reincarnation, soul, purpose of life, etc you would receive a remarkable series of replies. You cannot take such a poll because people do not feel able to give true answers to these questions.

That is our role and we are happy to be with you and to continue to influence you, with your permission.

63

THE GUIDING LIGHT OF MANKIND

We are coming to you now from a slightly different aspect. We are the spirit of mankind which has not yet infiltrated your consciousness; we represent the feeling of guidance you will experience in your roles and expectations. So if you want to choose a way to describe us, we are perhaps the guiding light. We are the aspect of mankind which provides a point to aim for, like a beacon on a hill. We will be able to give you a permanent feeling of direction.

Inevitably, at the end of a previous era, the guiding lights of that era have already been extinguished and now you are wallowing like a ship at sea with no lighthouse to aim for. You are thrashing about first in one direction and then the next, without knowing where to go, We hope to represent a new direction, or beacon, to aim for. As we become able to infiltrate our energy into your world, those who are ready to accept us will respond in a subtle way. We will provide you with a lovely feeling of purpose and direction which, after all, makes all the difference to one's life experience.

Perhaps the greatest thing now amiss with your society is a total lack of purpose or direction. In this country, life at the moment is good for most people; there is certainly unemployment, but are they starving? Most people have a modicum of health care, most people live in houses, most people have food and clothing, most people are able to spare a little money for the odd luxury, like a small radio to provide music for example, even if they may not have a television. But the problem is that because there is no sense of purpose these things have no relevance or appreciation. So, the physical well-being of the society is totally undervalued because there is no valid direction or set of values to give a person a feeling of self-worth or self-achievement. There is no bench mark to measure oneself against – no lighthouse to check whether you are going in the right direction.

We are that beacon which will provide people with a purpose and direction for the future. What is the purpose and direction? You have been told that new energy levels are initially those of discovering the commonality amongst mankind and then latterly with the world around you.

How can we provide you with a beacon to lead you to discover that you are more than just a series of individuals who happened to be dumped on this earth at random? We would suggest that a feeling of purpose, wholeness and commonality will follow from the realisation within society that life is not a one-shot deal. So, very simply, the recognition that people continuously reincarnate on earth, and the full understanding of the mechanics of that (not simply as a religious faith but with an understanding of the inevitability) will give a new perspective to the whole of their life.

So we would suggest that our main energies in the initial eras will be concentrated on bringing ideas about the continuum of life into man's understanding in general, but Western man in particular. That really is what we hope to do.

64

THE SPIRIT OF MANKIND I

We are the new mankind again. We have indicated before that we have a specific role to play, but now we wish to elaborate on it further. We are the spirit of the new mankind. There has been much debate about whether the future mankind will really be different from the mankind of the past. We say that there is a substantial and finite difference. It will be like the difference between a snail and a cucumber!

The new mankind will come into existence over a number of centuries. The mankind you know now is very different from those of former eras (thousands of years ago) – different physically and also psychically and at a vibrational level. The difference will only become physical latterly, but the fundamental difference is on another level.

During the next ten to twenty-five years, the young who come into this world will be quantifiably different from their predecessors. The differences will become progressive over five or six generations. You cannot expect it to happen all at once, because society would be split down the centre, There will be no comparison between the ultimate version and the original version, so it has to evolve prototype after prototype.

What is this fundamental difference? We will try to avoid woolly generalisations (which are in fact the truth). The first differences you can expect are in terms of psychic ability. All the psychic gifts will become very commonplace – mediumship, healing, psychokinesis, psychometry. All these things will become as commonplace as riding a bicycle or operating a computer is to the present generation. They will be the commonplace of daily life and people will think nothing of it because it will be so universal. That is the first step.

Secondly, these abilities will only become commonplace because there will be a sufficient level of responsibility to accommodate these things. They are powerful and dangerous when used incorrectly, so you can look for a quantum change in the level of responsibility in people's attitudes. The promised golden era refers to this willingness to take responsibility for concepts and ideas. This will have tremendous consequences. The consequences are, of course, that people will see themselves as guardians for the rest of the world, i.e. for mankind, and all the other interacting energies. Because the level of responsibility will exist concurrently, that will represent a most significant change.

Thirdly, you will also find much greater harmony amongst mankind; this probably follows from the second aspect because you cannot carry a level of responsibility for mankind in general and still harbour grudges, enmity and hate etc. In about three hundred years' time we are looking forward to a worldwide society (not just in one or two countries) where people actually have a noticeably higher level of tolerance, desire for peace, and understanding of other people's point of view. These will be still as varied as now – we are not expecting the world to suddenly become uniform, but the acceptance of other people's view of truth will be as natural as accepting that other people now speak foreign languages. One hundred years ago, foreigners might have been considered savages without the law. Today, we can see that evolution has changed and in future people will have a similar tolerance of other people's view of reality.

Finally, there will be a large amount of sourcing, just as you have been speaking with a source; so together with this higher level of responsibility will come a greater humbleness because of the knowledge that will be available. After about five or six generations this will create a great awe, and an overwhelming reverence for the source – the source being, of course, the same source that has produced all the other energies, the Earth in particular, the flowers and animals and everything else with it. This is the flip side of the change of attitude we expect to emerge eventually.

People have spoken of a golden age and in many respects it will be so, but the very fact that people will take this deeper and more philosophical view, with a level of responsibility and caring for the rest of mankind, will create its own problems. You may not have realised what these could be, but they will not be substantially different from the problems you face today. The problems today are, for example, how to reconcile conflicting needs to help humans to feed themselves. There is a very genuine desire to help feed people who are starving. That is an entirely laudable aim, but it may at the same time lead to despoiling our natural resources, like chopping down forests. That is a very real problem for you and we are not suggesting that one course is right and another is wrong – they are probably both undesirable, but you cannot now imagine anything other than a simple either/or situation.

Once you move onto a higher level you will be faced with similar paradoxes. Of course we say that everything is a paradox, but you will be faced with puzzles which you will be unable to resolve. Your perspective will be such that you will not see that you cause problems by either course of action. Those will be situations that people have to struggle with. They will be genuine struggles and there will be much debate with many contradicting ideas presented to resolve these situations, It may not lead to actual physical war, as in the past, but it could very well lead to a mental polarisation in spite of the fact (or maybe because of it) that people will have this wider sense of responsibility for the rest of mankind and the world around them. So again you see, you will still have paradoxical situations.

For example, with overpopulation, who is to decide that somebody should or should not have children; who is to impose their will on somebody else? What about the liberty of the individual? This illustrates in a graphic form the problems you will face – if you allow people the freedom of personal expression you cannot then turn around to them and say "You can only have one child". You either have freedom of expression or not.

In the future, people who choose to incarnate will come for the very reasons we have indicated. Those facets will be the things they come to develop; those who are not interested in developing those ideas will not find it worthwhile and will not bother to incarnate.

65

THE SPIRIT OF MANKIND II

We are another expression of the spirit of mankind. We bring you a new concept of mankind's role within the universe. The idea we wish to present is that of a confederation.

We would suggest that the role of mankind is like a federal state where the individual sections of the federation are linked together by one prime requirement, which is that the strength of the whole is greater than of the individual parts. Individually they are divided and easily knocked apart. United in this federal body they have a strength and a unison which makes them of consequence and it is their unity which is their most valuable asset. So what we are saying to you is that this federation of mankind is not understood.

Mankind perceives himself as in competition, or even at war, with himself. He cannot conceive that in modern society there is anything other than competition, whether it be economic or military or competition for space and resources, whether it be for fishing or polar research or space research – everything is seen in terms of competition. Well, we would suggest to you that there now needs to be such a fundamental revision of this philosophical approach that nothing less than total disintegration of the old idea will be acceptable. This has some pretty drastic consequences, because it actually means that people have to learn to voluntarily step back from their positions, from their advantages, from their strengths. This is certainly totally alien to the way in which the whole of Western society has developed, including the socialist as well as the capitalist countries. This requires a complete revision of the cultural basis on which your societies have been built.

Under the circumstances it is not very easy to change the philosophy of the last two or three centuries. In particular, at the moment there is quite a strong trend towards a reinforcement of that competitive instinct. We do not see any difference at all in socialist cultures compared with the capitalist cultures in terms of this competitive nature – they are as one. There is no difference in the fundamental philosophy – they simply have differences of achieving the same goals. And so we say to you that there needs to be a complete change, and the only way it can come about is by such a severe jolt to people's ideas that they will be forced to change their ideas to cooperation rather than competition.

I think you will understand that we are saying that mankind will inevitably receive some extraordinarily sharp reminders that they need to change their ideas. Once again we would emphasise that these dramatic upheavals are very positive, because they will achieve this end. This is the end you have been waiting for, and it is the entire purpose of your current incarnation on earth, so you must welcome the trauma, even though it causes great pain for most of mankind. The way you can help individually is to give perspective to people who do not understand what is going on.

We will give you the simplest example with the sudden emergence of the AIDS virus which has already started, and will become an acute threat to mankind. The threat will certainly be on the physical level, but it will primarily be on an emotional and a nervous level because of the fear and the suspicion it generates. You can understand when you think about the consequences to a society of fearing and suspecting a hidden cancer within itself – all the more feared because you do not know where it is. Imagine what that will do to the whole cultural structure of society. It is quite extraordinary that this could undermine the whole operation of society as you know it.

We would suggest that this is probably one of a number of things you will need to face up to and as individuals you can offer tremendous help and advice to people to understand the way things are developing. People will not necessarily accept what you say, but you can emphasise the positive aspects of these things. The positive aspects are that you need cooperation and the loss of this competitive environment.

POSTSCRIPT

We are one of the guiding forces for mankind. We are a nebulous energy. We are not even a character or an individual and we are certainly not human as such. We are a guiding force and a controlling force, but that is all we are. We are able to talk to you because this medium's guide has developed an unusual ability to communicate outside his human limitations, so he is able to merge with our thought-forms, and our energies, and thus receive the ideas which we generate and which we are implementing. Like this he is able to step beyond, himself. Similarly this particular channel is able to absorb the ideas which his guide has. So this guide is quite an unusual phenomenon and you should be rather happy that he is amongst you, able to perform these rather bizarre feats. The word 'channelling' describes the process rather nicely as it does not give any false sense of grandeur to the final mouthpiece – it is nicely understated.

Now that we are able to be with you in a new way, I would like to give you some encouragement, if you like. You have been meeting like this and sometimes you may wonder whether you are getting anywhere. We would like to suggest that you do not feel despair because what you do has a rather remarkable effect. There are situations where a thing needs to be done for the first time and once it has been done that activity generates a thought pattern, which can then be adopted by others – the "hundredth monkey" syndrome. You have stimulated a method, a thought-process and a way of working which can be tuned into by others and become part of the culture. The hundred-and-first monkey can then take it on board with remarkable ease. The first monkey has considerable problems. I can tell you that you are the first monkey.

What you are doing may seem difficult and irrelevant and tedious, but what you are forming is a brand new way of communicating. What you do now will form the prototype for the way other people will work in the future. So please accept what we say and accept also that the tediousness of the way you work has a tremendous long-term consequence. When in future years others are able to do it with ease it will be because of the template which you have formed in these early times.

66

THE ENERGY OF MANKIND

We are now able to come to you again. We are the energy of mankind, We have not been with you recently, but we are still here. Now we want to show you that you are part of a great scheme of things – a drop of the energy of mankind.

We want you to form in your imagination the idea of a radiant rainbow of energy encompassing mankind. Visualise this rainbow as a multi-coloured blanket surrounding the core of mankind, and visualise yourselves as one of the colours within the core, but also radiating outwards – you now form one of the colours within the complex spectrum of the rainbow.

Feel the particular power that you radiate, and know that it is true. Feel the importance of that colour within the spectrum of life, and realise that each band of colour is crucial to the formation of the whole – without it there would be a gap – and realise therefore that you are a crucial link in the chain of energies that form the totality of mankind. Feel the strength of your individual power, and know that you are central to the creation of mankind. As you sense the power, you form a crystallisation of the total life-force.

By your conscious visualisation of the whole, and the place of your individual colour within that whole, you are able to link with the whole and become one; and as you do that you represent the entire life-force within you, and not simply your own individual aspect. So you are both the strength of the individual, and a reflection of the totality. As you meditate on this, form the mental picture of your individual ray and the totality combined. That is the force of you, the life-force.

67

MANKIND'S ESSENTIAL SPIRIT

We are another version of mankind's essential spirit. We are not really part of the ordinary structure, We are somehow separate from mankind in his day-to-day life – we are like an overseeing force, the power which gives him the direction. The direction which comes to him through us is particularly important at this time of change. You might say that mankind appears to be completely lost at the moment, floundering about and feeling inadequate. That is probably only true of the older generation who were born for the previous era. The young on the other hand do have a very different attitude and potential and so it is really through the young that we, the "direction-changers", will try to operate.

Our connection is primarily with young people and we influence them in a variety of unexpected ways, through their music, through their physical activities, through their value systems, and through their culture (their culture really is a sub-culture to the main society). We are not really concerned with the development of the whole of mankind. If we can really influence the young up to the age of 25, we have done our duty, because from then on that age group will have formed its opinions and direction. Life is rather like rolling a ball down a skittle alley until it hits a skittle at the other end – we set the ball rolling. So we are the directors of mankind who are primarily concerned with the young.

When we work with them, we do so by insinuating new ideas, The ideas we are working with now are primarily those of human relationships. The human relationship aspect of the young is quite different from that of the old; they have ideas about human relationships which have a different meaning from the traditional rather tribal view. You will find that in the years to come their approach will be much more global. They will be able to form links with other people of like-minded spirit at will. They will not be limited to mixing only with the people they grew up with, or similar limiting criteria, which might have applied to the older generation. The new generation will have the ability to link with kindred spirits from any part of the world at a moment's notice.

So, it is really quite a different aspect. It is more generalised, in a sense, less specific, less limited, less family oriented, less tribal, but wonderful because it is so spontaneous and so universal. In the next twenty years the old barriers of culture, nationality and religion will really become quite irrelevant as far as the young are concerned. They will become more caring for the world, but not in the old exclusive mode. In the older civilisation you cared for your kith and kin almost exclusively. This new attitude will be much more open and it will involve caring for a wider spectrum of people. It may appear to be less intense or less involved, but this is not really so – it is because it is less exclusive. They will not only care for one individual but for great numbers. It may appear therefore that their caring is less deep, but that is an illusion, based on the previous generation's concepts.

The generation that is now between ten and sixteen will be the one to form the most significant change, so you can expect that within five years this age group will suddenly be coming to positions where they can influence things. They will be able to stimulate change, and that will be the time of greatest interest. In five years' time, someone who is now sixteen will be twenty-one and beginning to stir things up. It will be only for the good. They are the harbingers of change, but change for the good. I tell you nothing you do not know.

68

THE SPIRIT OF ENTERPRISE

We are about to bring a series of new connections and we are the first of the next phase of your contacts. The information is not for you alone – it is for all who wish it, all who are ready and can make use of it.

We are the spirit of enterprise. We are the hopes and aspirations of mankind. We represent the various achievements and failures that mankind has historically been responsible for. You should not dismiss these as mere blips in the passing of history, because they represent man striving towards his source.

Each era has its mainspring which gently winds down; each succeeding era has a major aspect which it attempts to resolve. We are responsible for the records of each era of evolution, each era of enterprise and endeavour.

Now, if you can understand the responsibility of each era you can begin to form a balanced picture of mankind. You will begin to see that mankind as a whole is the sum of all his achievements and failures to date. You are not individuals separated from that history. You are a direct result of that history and you have a direct role to play in the evolution of this next stage of development and in polishing the facet of the special areas involved.

So, my friends, over the coming weeks we will give you one or two aspects of different eras that existed in the past and which will come in the future. We hope that by doing this we will give you an understanding which you may not otherwise have had, because you are residents of a particular era. You cannot remember what the previous eras were like, but you are a product of them; we will give you an inkling of what it was like before and what it will be like in the future. My friends, until then, we have made our introduction and therefore we will take our leave.

69

THE SPIRIT OF MANKIND III

We are an old friend of yours; we are the Spirit of Mankind. As we represented ourselves before, we were concerned with the evolution of the spirit of mankind. When we came before, we spoke about the evolution of man, his historical connection and his future changes. The aspect that we wish to represent tonight is different – we wish to convey the feeling of man being a unity.

This idea (which has been expressed in other forms) is that having once developed as individuals you then need to learn to function without your individuality; you need to become 'at one' with the spirit of mankind again – that is your natural habitat. Certainly you need to learn how to link with the other kingdoms, but, as you recognise that growth involves reunification, you will realise that you need to reunite with the spirit of mankind.

This means that you must be prepared to lose your individuality, and this is a great challenge for you. By accepting union with the spirit of mankind, you learn how to let go of your own personality. When you gain the new knowledge, in the new environment, there will be a strong temptation to heighten the individual personality because of the increased power you will then have at your elbow. This will be a challenge, but true knowledge brings the realisation that individuality and personality are but a first step. The second step will require losing the conflict which the personality brings.

To achieve this you will need to learn to attune to the spirit that we represent – that spirit is the union of mankind, the essential nature of mankind, the core or the 'mankindness' of your own spirit. You therefore need to cultivate the recognition of your own 'humanness' as opposed to your individuality. Learn to recognise the common core of 'humanness' which links you with other individuals and with the common core and which forms the mainspring of mankind.

As the mainspring of mankind, we are not represented by any individual. We are the common core, we are the fount from which the spirit of man is drawn. Learn, therefore, to recognise your true spiritual home. Learn that you can reunite your essential core of 'humanness' at will. This is a very difficult challenge for you, but in order to take full advantage of the next phase of evolution, it will ultimately be essential. Learn to come home.

70

MANKIND'S PURPOSE

We come to you again with a different expression. We are the spirit of mankind and we have been to you before in a number of guises, but this is new. As the spiritual essence of mankind, we contain the kernel. That kernel is man's very purpose. The purpose of mankind is continuous – it does not change from year to year, it is not susceptible to the vagaries of evolution. That kernel is constant and unchanging. We are that essential ingredient. We are the spirit which contains the overview of man's development. We contain the very logic, the building blocks, of the genes of the human race. In a subtle way, we control the direction, the pace and the evolutionary nature of man's slow and painful progression.

I am able to talk to you now because we have reached a very significant moment. There are, as you know, many different eras but not every era has the same significance. We will say to you that about every twelve eras or so there comes a point when a very significant step has to be taken. We are now at that moment.

The change we are introducing to mankind will be slightly different, though comparable to the changes being brought to the other kingdoms. The change we are talking about will consist of an evolutionary double step. It is as though you will be taking two steps at once. The problem is that mankind is simultaneously resolving his earlier lessons about learning compassion, and at the same time he is trying to rediscover his connectedness and his roots – but that is only the first step. He also has to make the transition from being a self-seeking animal to becoming a harmonised animal. That is a dramatic, radical and totally revolutionary step.

Until now man has been fundamentally competitive. Until now his cooperation has been basically self-preservation – he would cooperate only in as much as it was in the interests of himself or the continuation of his species

– as an individual progenitor, shall we say. Now we have come to a point where he needs to learn that life exists on earth only as a reflection of life in the spirit. This is a dramatic step. In the spiritual life man understands that life cannot be competitive. Now, for the first time ever in this evolutionary period, he is beginning to learn that he must bring that spiritual awareness into his physical incarnation.

This will mean that the old animal instincts of competition and self-seeking for survival will have to be relearnt. This can only be achieved by abandoning most of what he has already learnt up until now. The process of abandonment will be traumatic, and total – root and branch.

I think you will now understand why man's adjustment to the new vibration is going to be so critical. Unless he can truly attune to the new vibration, he will remain unable and unwilling to throw away his old crutches. The new era will consist of learning that cooperation is the only true fulfilment. This goes totally against everything that he has learnt up until now.

My friends, you have a rather privileged position as you are being offered an understanding of the process and the reason for the change. This carries with it tremendous opportunities and also grave responsibilities. You have the opportunity to take this awareness out into the world, or you may choose to ignore it. I would just like you to bear in mind that a choice to ignore it will have a dramatic effect on your own personal evolution, understanding and progression. I do not mean it to sound like a threat – I am just saying that you have a unique opportunity, a great gift. For your own evolutionary future I would ask that you make the most of it, each in your own individual way.

71

THE ANIMAL DEVA

We are a new energy for you – we are not a human energy, but we can use human energy and intellect in order to communicate with you. Our source is deep within the animal kingdom. We are a controlling entity not related to any particular species. We represent the controlling overview of the whole animal kingdom. We control the rate at which species evolve and progress: which species are to be accelerated, and which are to be reduced; we are like a giant planning centre.

There is much concern in the world about the future of some species. We would like you to know that your concern is appreciated; it is always valuable to have human input into the condition of individual species. But we also want you to know that if one animal species comes to the end of its natural cycle, there will always be a new species ready to start a new cycle, albeit in a humble and unnoticed way, so we want you to know that you do not need to fear that in some way the world's animals will become defunct, moribund or even extinct.

You should know that there is a powerful controlling energy which is more powerful than any influence that man can bring about and it is able to nurture, control and stimulate the evolution and development of each species in turn as it proves necessary.

So we want to give you a word of reassurance and encouragement that the transitional period you are now experiencing will also be experienced by the animal kingdom and equally intensely. This will mean that some species will meet the end of their natural life-cycle. However, you do not need to become overly concerned by this natural evolution.

Some animal species will not be able to thrive in the new era which is about to commence. This is the reason that they now need to close their chapters. Other species will go through periods of intense evolutionary change. We will allow changes to take place that would normally have taken many thousands of generations to occur. In the future these changes will take place in as little as one hundred generations.

It is important to understand that the animal kingdom is the nearest and most vitally linked to the human kingdom – you are, after all, descended from the animal kingdom and you are dependent on it. But even more importantly, you represent a powerful role-model for the animal kingdom – your physical, emotional and psychic activities deeply influence the animal kingdom around you.

We would suggest that it is now time for mankind to become aware of the thought processes that he transmits to the animal kingdom. As man learns to refine his attitudes and thought transmissions, so too will the animal kingdom learn to respond in a new way to man.

This will bring them closer together. It will mean, for example, that you will be able to identify intuitively what each animal species is experiencing; you will understand the logic of evolution and the natural behavioural cycles to which it is bound. This will be an illumination for mankind, and the opening of a new era of deeper mutual involvement between mankind and the animal kingdom.

We come to you tonight to establish contact and to give you hope.

72

THE DEVA OF THE HONEY-BEE

We come to you with a special message. We are a new Deva, the Deva of the honey-bee.

We wanted to talk to you last night, but this is a good opportunity. We are delighted that you have the opportunity to work with us. We feel that this can be a wonderful exercise both for you and for us.

We would like to develop a cooperative exercise between the bee Devic forces and humans. It is an area which has been quite under-explored in the past and we would be delighted if you could develop this activity, and publicise it. We hope that you will start where you are living, and when you move, continue the experiment. We are happy that somebody has actually made the offer, and you will be able to communicate directly – both visually and also intuitively.

Bees, by their very definition, exist only as a group, and not as individuals, so you will always be talking to the group and not to an individual bee. As you talk to an individual you will simultaneously talk to the group; they are a good lesson for you humans. It is the way you should be. Humankind should exist as a unity. Perhaps you will learn the behaviour of the honey-bee and through publicising it will be able to draw parallels for human behaviour.

So, we are looking forward to being with you, we are delighted to have you join us. You will be astounded what you can produce, we will work well for you – you will win all the prizes!

We do hope you have enjoyed reading this book and have found the knowledge and wisdom within helpful.

Of all the many ways forward we can take in living our lives and in so doing growing our awareness, and therefore our consciousness, surely there can be no better way than by recognising that Source would, if asked, wish to experience life through...

LOVE